BREAKFAST BIBLE AND BULL

52 WEEKLY DEVOTIONALS FOR GUYS

DENNIS SWANBERG

FORWARD BY DR. BILL DYE

TABLE OF CONTENTS

CHAPTER 44
UNBREAKABLE –THE WINDOW CAN BREAK 241

CHAPTER 45
NO CARDBOARD FANS 246

# FOREWORD

I know of few people that have a better grasp of the unique issues Christian men are facing in this generation. The Swan has been doing ministry for over four decades now and during that time he's worked in every size church. When I came to North Monroe nearly twenty years ago Dennis was there to encourage and support me, but he also impressed upon me the vital importance of men, and ministry specifically targeting the men.

By the time our paths crossed, Dennis had already transitioned form the local pastorate to a national speaking ministry. But his roots and his heart were still firmly planted in the local church. And he helped me to see just how important men's groups were to the local church.

I don't know why its true, but men seem to be the keys to strong and healthy churches. Maybe women are just naturally more spiritual and they tend to be drawn to spiritual things. I don't know. But the Swan helped me see that if a church has a healthy ministry to the men, and if the men are standing on the

Word of God and living their faith in a transparent and authentic way then the church, families, and the community are far healthier.

Dennis is still connected to men from his former pastorate and those men are still reproducing their faith in the lives of a younger generation.   The fruit of Swan's passion and insights for men is still growing all over our community.

Dennis also knew something about the inner lives of men that I only vaguely understood. He knew how lonely most men are. He also knew that most men live with secret fears, regrets and sorrow that they are incapable of expressing.

I think it was Thoreau who said, "Most men lead lives of quiet desperation." Sadly, that's too often true of modern men. So few have anyone that they can turn to in times of trouble. Fewer still have a trusted confidant to share his deepest failures. Because of these hidden hurts and silent cries men are often left to soldier on alone and try to "man up" and deal with the hurts, sins, and setbacks on their own. They learn to weatherproof the façade and pretend that everything is fine. But inside things are not fine.

Like an infection that has been stitched over, those unhealthy pathogens are producing unhealthy spiritual consequences. Swan knew that men need men.

Dennis has been a champion of authenticity and transparency. When men find ways to share their pain they find healing and growth. He taught me that.

Swan also taught me the power of encouragement. Swan really is the "Minister of Encouragement."

I've felt it personally in my life. When I was at one of my lowest points Swan was there to encourage me and lift me up. He didn't come with threadbare cliché's and worn out platitudes. He moved into my life with the same pain and healing through which he'd personally walked.

Someone said, "Christianity is just one beggar telling another beggar where he found bread." For the last two decades the Swan has been sharing his bread with me. He usually dispenses it in our morning breakfast meetings at the local Waffle House. So "Breakfast, Bible and Bull" is nothing new for me. And that makes me so excited about this latest book. As you read these pages let it be your morning time at the Waffle House with the Swan. And my hope is that like me, you will walk away encouraged.

Dr. Bill Dye
Senior Pastor
North Monroe Baptist Church
Monroe, LA

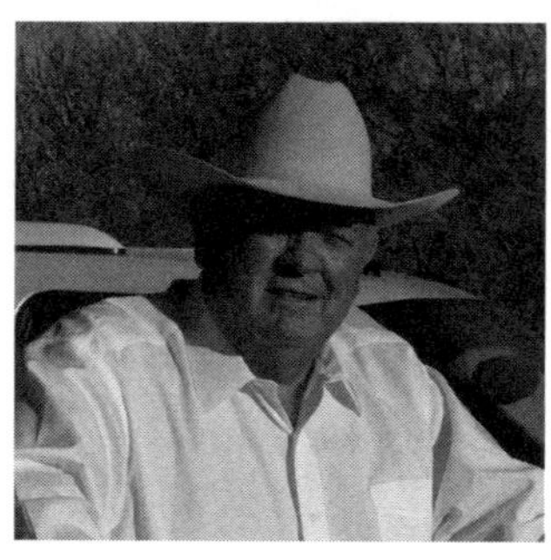

DEDICATION

This book is dedicated to the life and witness of my dear friend and big brother, Wade Freeman.

I grew up a middle child. Sandwiched between two sisters can have its advantages; yes, I admit I did pay my younger sister to make my bed and clean my room from time to time. But I always envied my buddies who had a big brother. There seemed to be a certain unspoken bond between them. As I got older and navigated my way through college, seminary and into the pastorate, I had many good buddies. Forever friends, great mentors, and guys whom God used to shape my life and speak truth into my personal spiritual journey.

The sanctuary at First Baptist Church Rogers, Texas was not a place where someone could hide. As I made my way through the side door that Sunday morning, I noticed 10-12 unfamiliar faces spread out among the crowd. With an average Sunday morning attendance of about 140, that meant only one thing…a pulpit committee from another church is there to "scout out" the preacher.

Scanning these new faces, I was immediately drawn to one man. He stood tall. Head and shoulders above everyone else. I likened him to James Arness that played the famous Matt Dillon in Gunsmoke. Or maybe a John Wayne character right out of the movies.

That was Wade Freeman. I didn't know it then, but I was looking at my new big brother. A man who would be in my corner for years to come.

Yes, Wade was the chairman of the pastoral search committee that led me to First Baptist Church, Saginaw, Texas. He and his precious wife, LouAnn, became not only dear friends, but also spiritual mentors to Lauree and me during my tenure there. Twelve years my senior, he believed in me, trusted me and followed me. He was a "pastor's man." He once told me "As long as you don't take money from the church cookie jar and you keep your britches up, I will follow you 100%." Not every pastor is fortunate enough to have someone that loyal and trustworthy.

Wade and I had many a meal together. He introduced me to Kincaid's grocery on Camp Bowie Boulevard in Fort Worth. A grocery store that served hamburgers so good customers didn't mind standing up to eat them. After we finished our burgers, Wade pulled out his "Stim-u-dents" (a brand of plaque remover tooth picks). Now, you have to realize the only other person I ever saw use a Stim-u-dent to pick his teeth was my Dad, Floyd Leon. Talk about an AHA moment! I knew then that our souls were blended and a spiritual brotherhood was born that would last for decades to come.

Lauree and I watched Wade and LouAnn raise two fine outstanding men. We saw the love and discipline they instilled in both their sons, Russ and Brad. Both of these men are a reflection of two truly remarkable people who invested their lives in shaping and molding them to be men of faith. I was honored to be part of both Russ and Brad's lives. They even were so kind as to ask me to officiate at their weddings. All these years it has been a joy to watch Russ and Carolyn and Brad and Marthanne as God has used them through their church, their business and their community. These two men have carried the legacy of their Dad into the marketplace and into the lives of countless others because of the godly example he set before them.

None of us was ready when God called Wade home in November of 2010. Having a career that took him to the top of his field with Texas Electric and the electric power industry, Wade had an influence in the business world and in the community of faith for many, many years. As I waited with the family before the funeral I was amazed again at the men and women that attended and honored his life. Business executives, friends, students, colleagues, and family who were there to honor Wade but also to show their love and support to LouAnn, Russ, Brad and all the Freeman family.

I miss my big brother, Wade Freeman. Even today, ten years later, it is still evident that the works of Wade Freeman follow after him in my life and the lives of many others. Revelations 14:13 says, ""Blessed are the dead from now on who die in the Lord! Yes, blessed says the Spirit, that they may rest from their labors, for their works do follow them". Amplified Bible Classic Edition (AMPC). And, because of the wonderful memories I have of Wade Freeman, I have gone on to having many more brothers in Christ. Wade taught me that even over a cup of coffee we could talk about spiritual things along with the struggles that each of us men face on a daily basis. We can't be so heavenly-minded that we are no earthly good. We were real and authentic, and we both experienced the reality of "iron sharpening iron."

He taught me to invest in the lives of men in order that they may reach other men for Christ. I can honestly say Wade and I shared a lot of breakfast, Bible and bull together. And, yes, he taught me that after any good meal, always have a good Stim-u-dent in your hand.

ACKNOWLEDGEMENT

Over all these many years, the Freeman family has been there for me, my family and our "Ministry of Encouragement." This book would not be possible without the generosity, affirmation and support of each of you. Thank you, Russ and Carolyn, Brad and Marthanne, and especially to the woman who always stood by her man, LouAnn Freeman: you are not just forever friends, you are family to us.

As Wade was a big brother to me, I hope in some small way that I can be a big brother to Russ and Brad. To carry on the legacy of a steady, wise, and faithful servant like Wade Freeman.

BBQ MEN – HEAT, MEAT, AND THE PIT

Did you ever notice that women don't barbecue? Now, I am sure there are exceptions to that. Somewhere in the good old USA, I am sure there is a lady standing outside in July when it is 110 degrees in Texas with smoke in her eyes and a sunburn. But that is not usually the case. Most like air conditioning. We men like smoke and sweat. There is just something rough, rugged and manly about a man and his grill.

You can always get into an argument about BBQ. Real grillers debate the wood (oak, mesquite, pecan, pinon, and others). They contest over the temperature for great brisket or pulled pork. They debate the amount of time as a factor of how much heat. There are advocates of stainless-steel smokers vs. brick (or in the Carolinas, a hole in the ground, watched by men who stay up all night fixing pulled pork and telling stories). Then there is the meat. East of the Mississippi, BBQ means pork. West of the Mississippi, it means beef. Added to that is the sauce or dry rub. There are even divisions in the sauce camps: mustard based, vinegar, and tomato based. If you go to Charlie Vergos' Rendezvous in a back alley on 2nd Street in Memphis, they will give you dry rub; you have to beg for sauce.

Whereas the ladies may discuss delicate recipes for meringue, it takes real men to discuss BBQ. It's just hard to imagine most men putting meringue on top of a little cake or a lady sitting up all night putting mesquite wood into a smoker at exactly 160 degrees. There may be exceptions, but there is no army of women watching a pig all night in a pit.

My mind works differently from most. Lots of things remind me of how the LORD works in our life. BBQ does that. In a strange way, stuff about BBQ reminds me of how God has worked in my life. Let me tell you about it…

Any pit master will tell you BBQ takes time. If you rush pulled pork or try to cook brisket too quickly, it just does not work. The same is true about God's work in our lives. He is not in a hurry. In fact, a day with him is like a thousand years and a thousand years like a day (2 Peter 3:8-9). God does not look at a watch, clock, or calendar. He has time. He does not have to rush what He is doing in your life. Did you hear about the man who cut three pet doors into his kitchen door? Someone asked him why he cut three pet doors into one good door. He replied. "I have three cats and when I want them out, I want them out now." God never acts like that. Like good BBQ, God has time to work on you. When God saves you, he knows every foolish thing you will do for the rest of your life. He is not in a hurry.

God also applies heat. "Do not be surprised at the fiery trial…" (1 Peter 4:12). BBQ pit guys debate the right amount of heat over time. There is no debate with the LORD about heat. You will face trials by fire. Ask Job. He lost everything and sat on an ash heap. Jesus never fooled His followers. He said it so you cannot miss it: "In this world you will have tribulation" (John 16:33).

He never said it was easy. If you are a certain age, you remember a song that Lynn Anderson and Glen Campbell sang in the 70s: "I beg your pardon, I never promised you a rose garden." A long time before Glen crooned that, Jesus said it about life. God uses heat and time to make you what He wants you to be.

He does it in different circumstances. BBQ guys debate stainless steel vs. brick pits. Sleek, expensive steel grills may set you back ten grand. You can build a brick pit for a hundred bucks and sweat equity. Some of you are very comfortable in life, but that can change. Others of you work three jobs and still don't make ends meet. God works in both cases. He does what He does with the up-and-outs as well as with the down-and-outs. No circumstance or context in your life can keep Him from working in your life. As the late Eugene Petersen wrote, Christ Plays in Ten Thousand Places.

God works in the McMansion and in the back end of the trailer park. Never tell God that He can't work exactly where you are. Stainless steel pits and brick pits are still pits, and He works in nice ones and not so nice ones.

Stop and talk to God right now. Don't try to compose some

high-sounding prayer. Just talk to Him the way you talk to your buddies: "Lord, I know I try your patience. I need you to take time with me. I have been a fool for a long time. Change me. Use heat if you need to. I know you can work on me anywhere. Please start where I am."

Pray this prayer every day this week. See you next Monday for more Bible & Bull.

PAUSE TO PONDER
I Peter 1:6-7

" ⁶ In this you greatly rejoice, even though now for a little while, if necessary, you have been distressed by various trials, ⁷ so that the proof of your faith, being more precious than gold which is perishable, even though tested by fire, may be found to result in praise and glory and honor at the revelation of Jesus Christ."

MONDAY

When and where did you have your first experience with BBQ?
Who is the BBQ chef in your family? If it wasn't your family's
experience – what friend of yours is the BBQ King? Think
back on those memories.

TUESDAY

How long has God been working on you? How does your life
resemble being on the Rotisserie of God's Grill?

WEDNESDAY

Take a buddy to your favorite BBQ place and enjoy some
fellowship. Maybe bring up some 'been-throughs" and "going-
throughs" from this week's devotional.

THURSDAY

What areas of your life need attention? What needs to be on
the back burner and what needs to be on the front with the
heat turned up?

FRIDAY

Spend time today letting God add His gracious but necessary
sauce to your life. Don't rush it! Have a good weekend –
maybe get some more BBQ – this time with the family.

SMART AS A TURKEY

Domestic turkeys are dumb but wild turkeys are smart. You might think exactly the opposite is the case. Turkeys that are coddled, kept indoors, fed special feed, and fattened up for Thanksgiving have had all kinds of turkey privilege. Outdoors, turkeys must avoid natural predators as well as reckless men shooting at them from behind camo. But that is not the case. How dumb is a domestic turkey? When it rains, he will look up with his mouth open and drown if you do not get him inside. A rainstorm at a turkey plant is a disaster. Wild turkeys know enough to keep their mouth shut.

For me it is easier to hunt anything else in the South. Deer blinds work. Duck decoys work. A good hunting dog flushes out quail. I can even hit a dove on a good day. Turkey hunting is something else. You wrap your gun with camo. You paint your face with camo. You download noises and practice with your turkey call. Then you go out and get behind more camo. Ants crawl up your pants. Hours go by. If you see a turkey, he is strutting 10 yards beyond where anything but a drone might get him. Wild turkeys have eyesight that make Clark Kent or Iron Man look nearsighted. If you blink your eyes, you scare them off into the next county.

I want to be as smart as a turkey. The devil has methods. That's why Paul used a word in his own language that meant methods. The old King James translates it wiles. You have a spiritual enemy. He walks to and fro in the earth. He is active. He is sly. If you've never read it, do yourself a favor and get C. S. Lewis's masterpiece, Screwtape Letters. It is the story of a master devil trainer who writes to his novice nephew, who is learning to tempt a new Christian.

Here is where the turkey comes in. Turkeys can spot you even when you have on camo. The tiniest glint of the sun off your gun barrel, the blinking of your eye, or your squirming when you find out you have set up your camo on an ant bed…any of it alerts a turkey. Our spiritual enemy always wears camo. He can transform himself into an angel of light. When the Devil comes after you, he never, ever looks like the devil. Let me tell you what he looks like.

Your neighbor's sweet wife is so understanding, sweet, kind, and innocent. You've been married to the same woman for 30 years. If there ever was any new, it has worn off. Your spouse tells you how your clothes don't match, how irritating your mother is, and asks you why you can't get a job like Oscar, her brother. Your neighbor, Mrs. Wonderful, on the other hand, always looks sympathetic, considers you the smartest human since Plato, and invariably walks over to compliment you when she is out sunbathing. She does not look like the Devil at all. He has horns; she has blond hair. He has cloven hooves; her toes are painted pink. He throws fiery darts; she brings you a fresh cold drink in July. She is an angel, not a devil.

She may indeed be as innocent as Mother Teresa. But your adversary knows how to ruin lives, bankrupt families, destroy two homes, turn your kids against you for the rest of their lives, shame you in church and your community, and then laugh at you while you die a lonely, miserable death. The Devil plays for keeps. That is a lesson you had best not learn yourself. You need to be as smart as a turkey. Spot him. Know that he always wears camo. He never, ever looks like what he is.

How can you be smart as a turkey? Stay out of range. The maddening thing about turkey hunting is that bird's ability to stay just out of range. I have seen them strut back and forth for hours ten yards beyond my shotgun range. They know how not to get too close. Do you catch my drift? Don't see how close you can get to temptation. Stay out of range. If you were hiring a driver to take on a treacherous road on the steepest mountainside, your ad would not read: "Driver wanted. Must be able to drive with one-half of the front and back tires over the outside edge of the road." That would be crazy! You would want someone who would hug the side of the mountain. You would rather ding the door than stay on the outside edge.

James, the younger half-brother of Jesus, puts it straight: "Resist the devil and he will flee from you" (James 4:7).

Denial works with the devil. Try it. When you want to get up in the middle of the night and look at a page on the web that would embarrass Hugh Hefner, deny him. Resist him. Tell him,

"You can go back to hell. You are not taking me with you." He will flee. Jeer at him. Mock at him. Tell him, "You have tried that stuff on me before. Don't let the door hit your tail on the way out." He will go.

PAUSE TO PONDER
JAMES 4:6-7

" *6 But He gives a greater grace. Therefore, it says, "God is opposed to the proud, but gives grace to the humble." 7 Submit therefore to God. But resist the devil, and he will flee from you."*

MONDAY

Find a Christian buddy. After the conversation gets warmed up over football and politics, change the subject. Ask him the dumbest thing the devil ever tempted him to do. Then you tell him the same.

TUESDAY

The first time the devil tempts you verbally rebuke the devil. Tell him to go to hell.

WEDNESDAY

Spend the day with one thought: Stay away from whatever tempts you. Do not even get close.

THURSDAY

As a variation, gently try to steer a buddy away from whatever topics, places, or habits would tempt him.

FRIDAY

Ask God to show you places in your life that you are vulnerable and do not even know it.

CHAPTER 3

PLAYING HURT

The second game and fifth inning of the 1951 World Series presented one of the most famous injuries in big league history. Joe DiMaggio and Mickey Mantle both tried to get under a fly ball. DiMaggio waved Mantle off. Mickey stopped quickly, stubbed his cleats into a sprinkler in center field, and tore up his knee. It was awful, serious, required many operations, and kept Mantle from being what he might have been for the rest of his career. Along with injuries it meant he played his famous career hurt, always and often in pain. Ted Williams, no beginner himself, thought Mantle would have hit 70 home runs in a season without the injury. Pain kept Mick from being what he might have been, but he was what he could be.

Mantle would also swing for the fences every time at bat. Even though the legendary Casey Stengel would order him to bunt or bat in a run, the slugger would swing for the fences every time at bat. He always thought he could hit a home run.

Life hands many of us the challenge to play hurt. We enter the game with childhood hurts, teenage hurts, dating hurts, professional hurts, marriage hurts, and hurts that we cannot even name.

Sometimes when I speak someone will say to me after the service, "Brother Dennis, you just don't understand my situation." They go on to tell me how their hurt is worse than everyone else's hurt and the only hurt like it that ever hurt in the way they hurt. I listen patiently. They are, however, wrong. Any way you are hurting belongs to categories of hurt that millions have felt across scores of centuries. The question is not whether you hurt, but whether you will stay in the game.

Abraham followed God, but hurt when his father died and when his nephew took the best land. Moses stayed in the game even though the people he was leading despised him and his own brother disappointed him. David stayed in the game even though his wife mocked him, his son hung himself, and his generals plotted against him. Hosea stayed in the game even though his wife Gomer became a prostitute. Peter denied, Thomas doubted, and John Mark went AWOL. They played hurt but they stayed in the game.

Mickey Mantle does not have anything on the men in the Bible when it comes to playing hurt. Paul himself indicated a hurt so deep he could not even tell us what it was (2 Corinthians 12). He asked God to take the hurt away, but God did not. He did give Paul more grace. The hurt was so bad that Paul called it a "stake in the flesh." The word "thorn" is too weak. It was as if someone spiked him with a metal spike. He had to live with it.

When you must play through pain you need to keep some things in mind. First, things will get better on the other side. The Apollo 13 disaster left the nation aghast. James Lovell, a.k.a. Tom Hanks, disappeared with his cohorts behind the moon. No one knew if he would fire the rockets at the right time, at the right angle, and for long enough to save the ship. There was no word from the dark side of the moon. When the three emerged and said hello to Houston, the whole world breathed a sigh of relief. Things were better on the other side. When the explorer Balboa landed in Central America, he and his men had no idea what was ahead of them. After a short march, they discovered the immense Pacific. They found out things were better on the other side. When Dorothy got home from Oz, she found out things were better on the other side of Oz.

The crypt of Mickey Mantle is at the Hillcrest Cemetery Mausoleum in Dallas. Fans from all over the world stand there and look at that immortal name. By direct report, not long before he passed Mickey came to Christ. My friend and Mickey's 2nd baseman Bobby Richardson made sure of that. He lived with pain but found out things were better on the other side. That is the ultimate answer for all of us. In this weary, wobbling world, things may or may not always get better on the other side here. The Christian faith promises things will indeed be better on the other side of time and eternity. The Irish speak of "thin places." Those are places where time and eternity seem to meet. Some of them are on the coast or in the green hills. To stand there is to almost reach through the gaze of time into eternity. All of us live at thin places. At any time, we may move to the other side.

PAUSE TO PONDER II
CORINTHIANS 12:7-10

" ⁷ Because of the extraordinary greatness of the revelations, for this reason, to keep me from exalting myself, there was given to me a thorn in the flesh, a messenger of Satan to torment me—to keep me from exalting myself! ⁸ Concerning this I pleaded with the Lord three times that it might leave me. ⁹ And He has said to me, "My grace is sufficient for you, for power is perfected in weakness." Most gladly, therefore, I will rather boast about my weaknesses, so that the power of Christ may dwell in me. ¹⁰ Therefore I delight in weaknesses, in insults, in distresses, in persecutions, in difficulties, in behalf of Christ; for when I am weak, then I am strong."

MONDAY

Identify by name the pain you are playing through. Give it
a specific name. Sometimes naming it hurts, but that is the
only way to get to the other side. If it is specific rejection by
a definite person, give it a name. If it is a moral failure, give it
a name. You must own who you are before you can get to the
other side.

TUESDAY

Remind yourself of times in the past when you played through
pain and got to the other side. You have; remember it.

WEDNESDAY

Ask yourself what keeps you from getting to the other side.
Habit? Inertia? Fear? Someone?

THURSDAY

Decide today the first thing you will get over, around, or
through to get to the other side. A difficult relationship, a
secret habit, or a deep bitterness?

FRIDAY

Now, help someone else get to the other side. Be honest,
loving, but blunt.
Sometimes you must carry someone over to the other side for
them to get there. Pick them up and carry them through.

WATCH - WHEN ALONE, TIRED, COMPROMISED, HURTING

IRS. NCAA. NFL. FBI. These are all acronyms. The letters stand for something that either strikes fear or suggests great enjoyment. Most of us look forward to the activities of the NCAA and NFL. Few of us want to be contacted out of the blue by the IRS or FBI. Acronyms can help us remember. Sometimes they can warn us. Consider SOS, which originally meant "Save Our Ship."

We need another acronym to help us remember when we are vulnerable. An astounding 20% of men admit to accessing porn at work. 40 million US adults visit porn sites regularly. There are 47% of Christians who claim that pornography is a major problem in the home. Ten percent of adults admit to internet sexual addiction. Guys, an astonishing 17% of women admit that they struggle with porn addiction as well.

The porn industry brings in a whopping $97 billion globally every year. This is more than all sports revenues combined.

Pornography results in human trafficking and by university studies leads to the breakup of romantic relationships. In Australia half of the very users of pornography indicated it had a "bad" effect on them.

So much of the time men find themselves alone, tired, compromised and hurting. Isolation leads to a lack of fellowship and that in turn becomes a lack of accountability. When men are alone and not involved in healthy activities with other men their minds often turn to sex. It just happens. When you add to that physical tiredness, your defenses are weakened and your focus is lost. Sometimes men are already compromised; they have been on phone chat lines or online chat or even secret visits to massage parlors. Recently a famous, rich person was found at just such a place against all explanation. He could have bought all such places in the city but visited one in a mall. The result was disastrous, embarrassing, and compromising. How many men could have been caught in the same situation?

I have an acronym to help us all with this mounting problem: **WATCH**.

When – There is a critical moment when you need to do just that, watch.

Alone – Premeditate those times when you are going to be alone. Get ahead of the curve. Have a prearranged plan. In a hotel room, put a Bible in front of the TV or on the work desk the moment you come in. Put a picture of your wife and family in your suitcase and get it out anywhere you stay. If you are alone in your car on a trip, deliberately listen to Christian podcasts and music. When the Son (and sun) comes out, the night disappears.

Tired – You are most likely to be tempted when you are physically exhausted. Make a covenant to go straight to sleep when you are tired, not ruminate on other things.

Compromised – You may already be in a situation that lacks integrity. Do not make a bad thing worse. Draw a line. Say no to the next step down the ladder to destruction.

Hurting – You will be hurt by your wife, kids, in-laws and co-workers. When you are hurt you must not turn to that which will only make you feel worse. Do anything that is positive and constructive. Think of Christian mentors, remember Billy Graham, consider your parents, anything that takes your mind away from the hurt. Check in with an accountability partner.

Remember, you can **WATCH**.

PAUSE TO PONDER
I Corinthians 10:13

" [13] No temptation has overtaken you except something common to mankind; and God is faithful, so He will not allow you to be tempted beyond what you are able, but with the temptation will provide the way of escape also, so that you will be able to endure it."

MONDAY

When will you be alone today? Prearrange one strategy that
will lead you in a positive direction.

TUESDAY

Find an accountability partner. If you cannot find one today,
start a conversation with a trusted friend that will lead to a
partnership in accountability.

WEDNESDAY

Stay away from houses, apartments. streets, strip centers, signs,
and any other places that pull you into a world that destroys you.

THURSDAY

When you are on the road, pack a small-framed picture of your
wife and children into your travel suitcase. Get it out and set it
up in a visible place. When you are at home or in your office
put a picture of your family on the desk or on your computer
screensaver. Make a conscious effort thoroughout the day, to thank
God for your family and loved ones. Call them each by name.

FRIDAY

Arrange a series of positive Christian messages, podcasts,
videos, and music that you feed into your mind when alone and
isolated. WATCH the heart back into yourself. WATCH the
heart into someone you know. Put heart back into a buddy.

LAWNMOWERS
AND PAPER ROUTES

In another world, like Star Wars, "long ago and far away," my buddies and I had to do things to get any money. The two most available remunerative jobs were mowing grass and throwing papers. The mowing and throwing routine did not make any of us wealthy trust kids. It did provide the possibility of enough change to go to the movie or later to take some young thing out on a date. Sometimes we had to mow our own grass in order to get an allowance. At other times we were entrepreneurs mowing other lawns in the neighborhood.

Paper routes were slightly more exotic. My buddy David Johnson had this prestigious employment. He threw the morning paper. Awaking out of a dead sleep at 3 a.m. in the morning, he met the grumpy old man who brought bundles of morning newspapers. Between 4 and 5 a.m., he would stumble down eight or ten blocks of sidewalks – yes, they did exist back then – and throw the paper on the front porch of the gripey old customers. The Lord forbid that he threw them where the sprinkler hit the headlines screaming the latest news about LBJ or Richard Milhous Nixon. Some mornings, I'm sure he was so tired that he did not care if either one of them got hit with the sprinkler.

Those days, however, put a little something into my generation that kids glued to iPhones do not experience. That is not to say that kids today do not have other productive habits. It is to say that there was something about blistering in the hot Austin sun mowing grass or freezing at 4 a.m. in the morning throwing 150 papers that has not been replaced. Of course. papers are going out of business weekly. And parents today pay other folks to mow their yards, people who came to our state willing to work just to be here.

I am grateful for the memory of mowing and throwing.

Some of you share these memories or something like them. Here is my question: What are you doing to give your kids or grandkids the same experience? I know. I sound like some grumpy grandpa pronouncing doom on civilization because of Millennials or GenXers. But folks, the verdict is in from across the country. You can read it in *The Wall Street Journal*. You can hear is on PBS. You can ask any human resources department in the country. The young workforce has a very different idea about work. A senior executive told my good friend that her accounting firm cannot find CPAs newly graduated from private or state universities who want to work enough hours to make partner. They have other goals. While millions of American kics live with their noses in a cell phone, millions of Asian kids are up before sunrise learning English to compete with our kids in a global market. It's tight but it's right. Don't kill the messenger.

I want to challenge the dads and granddads reading this. Make your sons get off their butts and work. Give them no choice to do chores, odd jobs, or retail. I am channeling James Dobson. You have a few years to instill into them the capacity to get up, wake up, and do something that makes them work. If they get mad at you take away the keys. Confiscate their phone. Lock up the XBox. Stop being afraid of your own son. What if he runs off? He can probably figure out that if he runs off, he will sure have to work more than he would if he stayed home.

The future of our nation depends on dads who know how to raise sons. My buddies who teach at universities are alarmed at the feminization of young men. They seem to have no clue what it means to be a man in any traditional sense of the word. This is not a misogynist statement. Women are taking places in our culture that are way overdue to women. They are leading corporations, presiding over schools, and flying planes. God bless them. May more of them do it.

At the same time, however, we are raising generations of boys who remain boys when they are still 40 years old. There is no guarantee that you will make a man out of your son if you do what I am saying, but there is zero possibility you will raise men if you do not do what I am saying. We need fathers today willing to be another Theodore Roosevelt. His sons, Theodore Jr, Archie, Kermit, and Quentin were models of manliness and discipline to an entire nation. Everyone knew the role Theodore played in raising them and everyone wanted their sons to be the brave, righteous, manly men they were. That was a little more than 100 years ago. How things have changed.

You may not agree with this but your discussion around my book this week will likely be lively and intense. If you think I am wrong just consider the outcome of doing the opposite or doing nothing. Without apology, I believe God assigned biological sex. What you were born with is what God intends you to have and to be. Anything other than that is a direct contradiction of Holy Scripture: "He created them male and female" (Genesis 1:27). That does not mean men cannot do traditional feminine things and women can do traditional male things. That is happening. There are stay-at-home dads and working moms. Let the Lord use them. At the same time, our western civilization did not invent the God-given nature and roles of biological males and females. Those natures are assigned by the very will of God in the Bible. For that matter, most guys with any common sense know that, Bible or not.

Let's commit ourselves to raising sons and grandsons that exemplify the disciplined life of real men.

PAUSE TO PONDER
PROVERBS 3:6-12

"In all your ways acknowledge Him,

And He will make your paths straight.

7 Do not be wise in your own eyes;

Fear the Lord and turn away from evil.

8 It will be healing to your body

And refreshment to your bones.

9 Honor the Lord from your wealth,

And from the first of all your produce;

10 Then your barns will be filled with plenty,

And your vats will overflow with new wine.

11 My son, do not reject the discipline of the Lord

Or loathe His rebuke,

12 For whom the Lord loves He disciplines,

Just as a father disciplines the son in whom he delights."

MONDAY

Ponder today what you can do with your son or grandson that demonstrates traditional, wholesome manly virtues. This does not have to be hunting or fishing or camping, but it may be. Do something with him that shows discipline, independence, initiative, and a milligram or two of testosterone.

TUESDAY

Help your son find some manly reading. There is nothing wrong with literature such as Ernest Hemingway's Old Man and the Sea or Jack London's Call of the Wild. For a change, look up Ken Burns remarkable documentary on World War II as he follows boys from four towns throughout the war. If you don't like that one, look at Kens documentary, Baseball.

WEDNESDAY

At the same time, show your son that he can also do things to help mom. Teach him to wash some dishes, iron his own shirt, and sew on a button. Our sons need to know a combination of virtues, not just one role. Teach him to shoot a turkey one day and make a casserole the next, not one without the other.

THURSDAY

Get some boys together and take them to do something traditionally male. You pick it.

FRIDAY

Find a boy without a father. In a gentle and appropriate way, encourage his mom to let you take him along with your own son. There is absolutely no end to the good that will do, both for the single mom and her son. Above all, teach him gentle, manly respect for his mom.

IN THE FIRE

As a Texan, one of my boyhood heroes was Red Adair, the famous Houston oil well firefighter. He put out more than 2,000 oil well fires. I remember watching the 1968 movie when John Wayne played a character based on Adair, *Hellfighters*. Me and my buddies looked at Adair as a man's man. Remember when your elementary teacher asked the boys what they wanted to do when they grew up? I bet you 50% of your class said they wanted to be a fireman. There is something raw, brave, and daring about fighting fires, then and now.

The Old Testament prophet Daniel wrote the most curious firefighting story ever (Daniel 3:19-30). Daniel's three friends, Shadrach, Meshach and Abednego, had been robbed of their godly Hebrew names and given those three ugly Babylonian names. It would be like renaming Bubba Jones after a Ninja Turtle. Nebuchadnezzar tried to cancel their very identities. The world does that to believers. When the three lads refused to bow down to an idol that looked like Nebuchadnezzar, he went ballistic. He heated up an incinerator seven times hotter than it had ever been. He tied the trio up and had them thrown into the incinerator. The guys who threw them in were burned up even throwing them in. Shadrach, Meshach and Abednego were toast; but then again, they were not.

When Neb investigated his personal oven, he saw the three boys not only unbound, but walking around like they were on a beach in Florida or Mexico, taking in the sun. That's not all he saw. He saw a Fourth Man in the Furnace (Daniel 3:25). That Man looked like a God. The early church writers thought the Fourth Man in the Furnace was a cameo appearance of Jesus. Even Red Adair could not put that fire out.

Rugged old Peter wrote early Christians about the fire. He urged them not to be surprised at fiery trials as if they were something strange (1 Peter 4:12). Much of the Christian life is lived in the fire. Jesus endured the worst fire of all, the Cross. Paul spent seven years in jail and was then beheaded. James was thrown into jail and then executed. Tradition tells us that all the Twelve except John the Beloved were martyred. John himself spent his last days as an old prisoner on the tiny island Patmos. The first 300 years of the Christian faith witnessed great waves of persecution by Rome. Trials came in like the tide and carried Christians out to the sea of eternity by the boatload. Martin Luther spent his adult life kicked out of the Roman church and banned by the Empire. Calvin was run out of Geneva. John Knox was chained to the oars as a galley slave, just like Charlton Heston in *Ben Hur*. Bonhoeffer was executed April 9, 1945, a few days before the Allies would have liberated him. More Christians have died for the faith in the

20th century than any century since ancient times.

Yet you and I think we are in the fire if someone at work jokes about us because we believe in Jesus. A snarky co-worker jokes that you talk to an invisible friend named Jesus like Jimmy Stewart talked to the invisible rabbit in *Harvey*. A godless cousin snipes at you at Thanksgiving dinner, reminding you of fallen preachers and Christian fakes. A partisan person mocks your faith in the midst of politics or a pandemic. The guys on a business trip mock you because you will not go to a strip joint. These are just little flames compared to the big fires of Christian history. The harder fires are those of betrayal in your own home, devastating diagnoses, and runaway kids. God never guaranteed you would not face flames and conflagrations. In fact, Jesus flatly stated, "In this world you will have tribulation" (John 16:33). He flat-out promised it. You will live in a fire much of the time.

Here is His deal. He will not save you out of the fire, but He will walk with you in the fire. You will never find Him closer than when you are in the fire. The heaviest end of the Cross falls on His shoulders, not yours. He will stand in the thickest part of the battle and the hottest part of the fire. Look for Him and you will find Him.

There is a radical misrepresentation of the Christian faith rampant today. That counterfeit promises you health and wealth if you have enough faith. That is just an outright lie. Ask Job, a man so righteous that God bragged on Job to the devil. Job lost his stuff, his kids, and his own health. In the middle of that he was surrounded by "friends" who told him it was all his own fault.

They threw gas on the fire. Yet at the end of the book, it is God who stands with him in the fire. There is no "solution" other than the presence of God and His final blessing on Job at the end of the fire.

The old hymn writer put it this way:

When through fiery trials, the pathway shall lie;
My grace, all-sufficient, shall be thy supply;
The flame shall not hurt thee; I only design;
Thy dross to consume, and thy gold to refine.

God has a purpose in your fire. It is to refine you in ways that nothing else can do. In Jeremiah 18, the prophet saw a potter turning clay at a wheel. He mentions the wheel, the clay, and the potter. Yet we know nearby was one other thing, the kiln. Unfired clay is limp and useless. It takes the fire to bring the use. So it is also in life.

PAUSE TO PONDER
I Corinthians 3:12-13

" 12 Now if anyone builds on the foundation with gold, silver, precious stones, wood, hay, or straw, 13 each one's work will become evident; for the day will show it because it is to be revealed with fire, and the fire itself will test the quality of each one's work."

MONDAY

Face your own trials. Call them what they are. Look straight
into the fire.
Admit the people, places, and situations that are fire in your
life. Call them out before God. Then give them to Him.

TUESDAY

Look for evidence that Someone is in the fire with you. There
is always the Lord there, who even though invisible, at times is
more real than any other.

WEDNESDAY

Sort out your fiery trials. Some of them you ignited yourself
and some were caused by others. It will help you to note the
difference between burning yourself up and someone else setting
you on fire. Ask God to forgive you for the fires you started and
to give you endurance in the fires you did not deserve.

THURSDAY

Remember past fires and the way God delivered you. The fire
did not last forever, did it?

FRIDAY

Find someone else in the fire today and help that person see
the One in the fire with your friend. Everybody around you is
in some fire and needs encouragement. It will help you put out
your fire if you help someone else in his fire.

THEY GOT US SURROUNDED

If you are a fan of the old westerns, not the fancy new ones but the old ones filmed out in Arizona, you remember the line, "They got us surrounded." That was a repeated phrase when the cowboys were surrounded by rustlers or banditos or rightly offended Native Americans. It meant there was no escape because enemies were all around them. For the person of faith, to be surrounded has another sense altogether. When Elisha was hiding in Dothan (Israel, not Alabama!), his servant awoke to see the city surrounded by Arameans, the enemies of God's people. The alarmed servant asked Elisha what to do. The prophet gave a memorable answer:

"Do not be afraid, for there are more with us than there are with them." Then Elisha prayed, "O Lord, please open his eyes that he may see." So, the Lord opened the eyes of the servant, and he saw; the mountain was full of horses and chariots of fire all around Elisha"

(2 KINGS 6:16-17).

To be a person of faith is to believe in the reality of unseen spiritual personalities, invisible to the human eye, but eternal and real. When Paul was alone in Corinth, the LORD appeared to him in a vision and assured him that God had many people in that pagan city (Acts 18:9-10). If you have a red-letter Bible, those words are red right in the middle of Acts; it was a cameo appearance of the Lord Jesus Christ. Hebrews 13:2 famously warns us to be hospitable, because sometimes you entertain angels and are not aware of it. God has unseen and mysterious personalities at His disposal at all times.

For the believer, this world is surrounded by invisible personalities of good and evil. The imprisoned Paul wrote about the evil personalities: "For our struggle is not against enemies of flesh and blood, but against the rulers, against the authorities, against the cosmic powers of this present darkness, against the spiritual forces of evil in the heavenly places" (Ephesians 6:12). I can testify that not one, but two, presidents of a major Christian university confessed they were in such a battle with darkness trying to possess the soul of the university. The powers of darkness and light are invisible, but they are real. What are you to make of this in your life?

Recognize that you are in a battle, not in a recliner. We best be aware that there is a spiritual battle for our souls every day. C.S. Lewis caught the gist of this in *The Screwtape Letters*, where a seasoned tempter advises his nephew freshman demon how to ruin a young Christian. We are not to be casual about this. The great Christian All Pro defensive end for the Cleveland Browns (decades ago), Bill Glass, warned Christian men not to be casual about Christian living: "If you are casual in the NFL you will get knocked on your casual can. That is also true in the Christian life." Be intense in the spiritual battle. The late famous preacher, Stephen Olford, used to read Ephesians 6 every morning and put on each piece of the Christian armor with prayer (Ephesians 6:13-20).

Confess that the invisible force of light will overpower the forces of darkness. We are not to battle as if the outcome were in doubt. Just as the allies knew the Germans were defeated after Normandy, but still had to fight their way through France one hedge row at a time, we are in a winning battle, but a battle it is and there can still be casualties.

What a sadness to quit the battle in a war where you are on the winning side. Fight on. For one thing, rebuke the devil and he will flee from you (James 4:7). When the enemy of your soul comes after you with anger, lust, compromise, pornography, or lewdness, rebuke him. You will be surprised at the result. Tell the devil where he can go. I am not kidding. We tell the wrong people that. We cannot send another human there, but we have every right to tell the devil to go home. Tell him, "Burn baby, burn." He will depart until a more convenient season. You are on the winning side but do not quit the battle.

PAUSE TO PONDER
Ephesians 6:13-20

" ¹³ *Therefore, take up the full armor of God, so that you will be able to resist on the evil day, and having done everything, to stand firm.* ¹⁴ *Stand firm therefore, having belted your waist with truth, and having put on the breastplate of righteousness,* ¹⁵ *and having strapped on your feet the preparation of the gospel of peace;* ¹⁶ *in addition to all, taking up the shield of faith with which you will be able to extinguish all the flaming arrows of the evil one.* ¹⁷ *And take the helmet of salvation and the sword of the Spirit, which is the word of God.*

¹⁸ *With every prayer and request, pray at all times in the Spirit, and with this in view, be alert with all perseverance and every request for all the saints,* ¹⁹ *and pray in my behalf, that speech may be given to me in the opening of my mouth, to make known with boldness the mystery of the gospel,* ²⁰ *for which I am an ambassador in chains; that in proclaiming it I may speak boldly, as I ought to speak.*"

MONDAY

At the beginning of the day, affirm out loud that God is
with you and you are surrounded by invisible forces of light.
Remember that all day.

TUESDAY

Today rebuke the devil in a specific situation. Hold up the
blood of Jesus in his sooty face and tell him to where to go.

WEDNESDAY

Identify somewhere today that you sense the powers of light
and the powers of darkness. You can see them with the eyes
of faith if you look.

THURSDAY

Start today like Stephen Olford. Read Ephesians 6 and put on
the whole armor of God.
Sing the words of the great old hymn, "Stand Up Stand Up for
Jesus": *"Put on the gospel armor, each piece put on with prayer;
where duty calls or danger, be never wanting there."*
We have a lot of wimpy, snowflake Christianity today.
Be a soldier.

FRIDAY

Turn your face away from the mirror and help someone else
who is struggling. Help him to know he has help he cannot see.

CHAPTER 8

SIDE GIGS: YOU CAN DO MORE THAN ONE THING

Tom Clancy was an insurance adjuster. He also loved writing about weapons and war. In his spare time he wrote a naval novel, *Hunt for Red October*. He could not find a publisher. Finally, a little specialty press published the book. It vaulted him into international fame, resulted in a famous movie, and began a career as an author. The same was true of an Oxford, Mississippi lawyer named John Grisham. He could not sell his first novel, *A Time to Kill*. Then he wrote another one called *The Firm*. It exploded onto the scene and the young lawyer became an overnight sensation.

At 50, Julia Childs did not know what she wanted to do. She had worked as a spy during World War II. and had taken cooking lessons while her husband Paul was stationed in France. Then one day, on a local PBS station in Boston, she brought a pan, a Bunsen burner, and awkwardly cooked an omelet on TV. That is the most consequential omelet in history. People went nuts over the tall, ungainly lady whose voice sounded like scratching your fingers on metal. Truett Cathy came back from the war and wondered what to do. Everyone else was selling hamburgers. He decided to sell chicken sandwiches in a tiny Atlanta diner. We all know how that worked out.

Someone said that a rut is a grave with both ends kicked out. Life can put you in a rut. The same ritual becomes so commonplace that you never even think about doing anything else alongside what you are doing. A famous poet wrote the noted lines about a man who lived in a rut: "Mornings, evenings, afternoons; measuring out life by coffee spoons." You can get caught in the same old same old.

Look at the first followers of Jesus. Four of them worked as commercial fishermen. Then Jesus walked by and told them to follow Him. They had been catching live fish and selling them when they were dead. He would make them catch dead men and bring them to life. Matthew worked for the IRS. What a change in jobs he experienced! Simon the Zealot was a member of a gang that wanted to kill people like Matthew. He quit the gang and followed Jesus. You would never have heard of any of them if they had not taken on a side gig of being a disciple of Jesus.

Now, don't get me wrong. Please don't go to the office and tell them to forget this job. To consider doing something alongside what you are doing is not the same as jumping off a cliff. Anthony Trollope spent his entire life working for the UK post office in the 19th century. He even invented the famous red post box in the UK. Yet at 45, he became a famous novelist beloved by millions then and now, second only to Charles Dickens. Even when he was a wealthy author, he never quit the post office. He would be paid as much for one novel as he made all year at the post office. He lived parallel lives and enjoyed it immensely.

Have you ever considered a side gig? I do not mean that you become a workaholic; that creates other problems. Yet you can find measured, fulfilling, other things to do. It spices up life, adds zest to your years and gives meaning. The longshoreman philosopher Eric Hoffer worked the docks and at the same time became a serious writer. He won the Presidential Medal of Freedom in 1983. What a side gig. Unload ships and write moral philosophy at the same time. He went from the ships to Socrates.

Such a two-lane life is not for everyone, but it might be for you. At the very least, follow some other passion. It is common in the UK for every man to have a vocation and an avocation, a hobby. Collect fountain pens. Join a local association of enthusiasts for whatever. A friend was afraid of flying, so he conquered it by becoming a pilot. Try the Nike slogan: Just Do It.

PAUSE TO PONDER
ECCLESIASTES 3:1-8

"There is an appointed time for everything. And there is a
time for every matter under heaven—
2 A time to give birth and a time to die;
A time to plant and a time to uproot what is planted.
3 A time to kill and a time to heal;
A time to tear down and a time to build up.
4 A time to weep and a time to laugh;
A time to mourn and a time to dance.
5 A time to throw stones and a time to gather stones;
A time to embrace and a time to shun embracing.
6 A time to search and a time to give up as lost;
A time to keep and a time to throw away.
7 A time to tear apart and a time to sew together;
A time to be silent and a time to speak.
8 A time to love and a time to hate;
A time for war and a time for peace."

MONDAY

Do you have any compelling interest other than your job?

TUESDAY

If you were to look for an outside gig, what would interest you enough to risk it?

WEDNESDAY

What could be the worse outcome if you tried something else alongside what you are doing?

THURSDAY

When you are completely retired, will you be satisfied that you only did what you are doing?

FRIDAY

Ask a friend who has developed an avocation, hobby or 2nd calling. Let him sharpen your thoughts. Remember, iron sharpens iron.

A MAN AND HIS STUFF:
YOU CANNOT MAKE DIRT

The man had a little soul and little barns. The Rich Fool is one of Jesus' most memorable stories (Luke 12:13-21). The great preacher Haddon Robinson imagined the man in his wooden wainscoted study looking at blueprints for bigger barns. On the wall were three plaques: Bethlehem Farmer of the Year (A.D. 30), All Judea Farmer of the Year (A.D. 31), and All Israel Farmer of the Year (A.D. 32). A man like that needs bigger barns! By the lamplight he squinted at the architect's rendering of magnificent barns. He would tear down barns that caused envy in his neighbors and build still bigger barns. At about 8 p.m., there was a knock on his door. He looked at his Outlook Express and he had no appointments. A presence haunted the room even though the door never opened. "Ten, nine, eight...."

"Take my barns; I don't really have to have them," the farmer shouted into the air at an unseen Somebody.

"I have no need of barns," the spectral figure responded. "I have come for you. Seven, six, five, four…."

"Take it all, everything. Leave me alone," the terrified farmer responded. "Three, two, one…."

They found the majestic barn planner cold and dead over his barn blueprints the next morning. The last thing his silent ears had heard began with the word, "Fool."

Often missed in this parable are the first words: "The ground of a certain rich man yielded plentifully…." This self-congratulatory agrarian misunderstood the first, most basic reality of human life. Everything we have is first a gift. A farmer depends on crops. Crops depend on seeds, which no person has ever made. The seed must take root in dirt, another thing no person has ever created. Dirt takes millions of years to form. Ask the famous Joad family leaving Oklahoma in the Dust Bowl disaster if a mere man can make dirt? The life of every person inhabiting this planet depends on dirt. When the thin topsoil blows away no farmer can grow anything. Dirt is a gift. Every seed that sprouts depends on dirt or something else growing in dirt.

We use the phrase, "Dirt poor." We would better say, "Dirt rich." Only God and millions of years can make dirt. The thin layer of that mysterious stuff cannot be made by humans. Humans might try to make a small amount *by taking other elements humans cannot make and combining them.* Humans can only combine what is already there.

You don't like dirt? Then think of petroleum. The world we

occupy craves petroleum in the air, on the ground, and under the sea. No human has ever made a barrel of crude oil. No atomic engineer, no chemist, and no inventor can make a single barrel of crude oil. Like dirt, oil is a gift. In the 19th century, the famed preacher Henry Parry Liddon stood in amazement at the greatest building of that century, the Crystal Palace in London. It stood for the zenith of human achievement. Yet Liddon noted that no human could make the smallest insect that landed on a piece of the brilliant glass walls. Humans can only recombine what is already here. We cannot make the primary.

This was the first and biggest mistake of the little man with even smaller barns. He forgot that the ground yielding plentifully was a sheer gift from God Himself. He could build barns, but he could not make seeds. He could plant seeds, but he had to have dirt. Trace any human provision or need to its origin and it reveals something humans cannot make. To breathe you need air, but you cannot make lungs or air. To satisfy thirst, you need water, but you cannot make the water you need.

That is why the bragging of the barn-loving rural fool hits a snag. No dirt and there is no harvest. He could not make the most basic stuff he needed to fill bigger barns, dirt. This parable is a warning against covetousness, wanting more and more of what you already have enough of.

The first line of defense against covetousness is the understanding that everything that sustains our lives is a gift. God is the giver. When you see all of life as a gift rather than an entitlement, it will change your perspective. You will not obsess over more and more of what you already have enough of. You will thank God for dirt, and other stuff He gave, without which your life would not last a minute.

"If it were his intention and he withdrew his spirit and breath, all mankind would perish together, and humanity would vanish into dust" (Job 34:14-15). You are only here because He gives you your next breath. Ask Steve Jobs, if you could.

PAUSE TO PONDER
MATTHEW 6:33

"But seek first His kingdom and His righteousness,

and all these things will be provided to you."

MONDAY

Be hard on yourself for a minute. How much of what you
expect from life do you expect as an entitlement rather than a
gift? Name the stuff.

TUESDAY

Consider in your field, whatever that field is, those things that
make it possible, things that are provided only by God, stuff
that you cannot make.

WEDNESDAY

Plead with God to give you gratitude for your existence,
energy, and very being.

THURSDAY

What plans do you have that do not depend on what only
God can provide? What do you plan to do, where do you
intend to go, and how do you think you will have the time to
do it or go to it? Those are all in the hands of God.

FRIDAY

Find a brother to be an accountability partner at the point of
your dependence on God for your business, plans, finances,
family and the next hour God gives you.

CHAPTER 10

FORGET YOURSELF

The verdict is already in. The greatest theologian of the 20th century was Karl Barth. He was a juggernaut of productivity. He wrote tens of million of words. His fame circled the earth. Yet Barth never took himself that seriously. Once he was on a bus in Basel, the city where he lived and worked. A tourist hopped on the bus and sat down next to Barth. The famous theologian asked the traveler what he came to see in Basel. The unknowing tourist told Barth that he had come to see the famous theologian Karl Barth. He then asked Barth if he knew Barth! Barth answered that he shaved Karl Barth every morning. The amused tourist left, telling everyone that he had met Barth's barber.[1]

In more than once instance, Barth demonstrated a healthy sense of self-forgetfulness. That is the very opposite of what a friend recently saw on a plane. My friend was on a late-night flight. Unusually, the jet was mostly empty. A woman entered

---

1 Eugene H. Peterson, *A Long Obedience in the Same Direction: Discipleship in an Instant Society*, rev. ed. (Downers Grove, Ill, 2000), 196.

the plane with her male friend. He left her in first class. He went to the back of the coach class. The attractive lady asked the flight attendant if her friend could join her in first class. The attendant, following the rules, reluctantly but firmly said, "No." The lady quietly agreed. Now, here is the kicker. The plane was nearly empty. She could easily have sat next to her friend in coach. All she had to do was get up and go back to coach. She did not do that. She was far more impressed with her first class seat than wanting to demote herself to sit with her friend.

These two human stories contrast self-forgetfulness when you would not expect it with narcissistic self-consciousness when you would not expect it. There is something about the best folks in life that is willing to forget self. It is a conscious forgetfulness. Such men do not stop, think, and tell themselves, "I need to forget myself in this situation." That is no more the case that a rose would say to itself, "I need to smell fragrant today." It just comes naturally.

Senator Daniel Inouye was a great American hero and a famous six-term member of the United States Senate. In World War II he was leading his troops in a European battle when shrapnel cut into his flesh and almost severed his arm. Rather than retreat and against the calls of his astonished troops, he surged forward directly into the line of fire, pried a hand grenade out of his severed hand with his other hand, lobbed it into a German pillbox and kept on fighting. He had to be dragged off the battlefield in his self-forgetfulness. Little wonder that he spent decades as a national hero.

The Lord Jesus Christ is our great model in self-forgetfulness. Philippians 2 tells us that even though He was in the form of God, He emptied Himself and took upon Himself the form of a servant. Our very gospel depended on a Lord that did not insist on His prerogatives or cling to His position. He went from an eternal oneness with the Father to a very real stable and then a carpenter's shop in a tiny town. No being in all eternity was more self-forgetful.

We all know folks who are full of themselves. Theodore Roosevelt's daughter Alice had a love-hate relationship with her father. She once stated that Teddy wanted to be the bride at every wedding and the corpse at every funeral. Even though she loved her daddy, that was not a compliment.

Someone noticed that a certain general walked into his outer staff offices pointing to his stars in order to show his rank. When you have to point to your stars you really are not one. There is something about real leaders that does not have to insist on leadership by pointing out what a leader they are. If you have to go into the office every morning screaming, "Now hear this…I am the leader," you are not.

I will wager you that the people you most admire in life had a habit of self-forgetfulness. They were able to focus on others rather than themselves. They did not have to crow about their accomplishments or remind you of their rank or position.

PAUSE TO PONDER
Philippians 2:5-11

"Have this attitude in yourselves which was also in Christ Jesus, [6] who, as He already existed in the form of God, did not consider equality with God something to be grasped, [7] but emptied Himself by taking the form of a bond-servant and being born in the likeness of men. [8] And being found in appearance as a man, He humbled Himself by becoming obedient to the point of death: death on a cross. [9] For this reason also God highly exalted Him, and bestowed on Him the name which is above every name, [10] so that at the name of Jesus every knee will bow, of those who are in heaven and on earth and under the earth, [11] and that every tongue will confess that Jesus Christ is Lord, to the glory of God the Father."

MONDAY

Who is your favorite theologian or Bible teacher?
What makes them special to you: message, style, illustrations,
and/or applications, or is it their personality?

TUESDAY

What is your definition of humility? Write down three of the
most honorable people you know.

WEDNESDAY

Do you have a national hero? Did humility have a place in
their life? Or would you say they have a confident humility?

THURSDAY

Write down two or three stories of Jesus' personal life that
have left a legacy of humility.

FRIDAY

One of my heroes in the faith once said, "It's almost impossible
to offend a humble man." What do you think about
that statement?

CHAPTER 11

LIVING LIFE WITH THOMAS CRAPPER

There are several words for the same human reality. The formal word is *excrement*. The old King James Version calls it *dung*. You probably could think of some other descriptive words. Yet Thomas Crapper, an Englishman who invented the most successful commercial toilet, gave his name to it as well. Most men must swim through a great deal of it in daily life. That is the reality of life in this world. In another book I published, *No More Secrets*, I referred to this illustration as well. In light of Crapper's invention, I think it is worth repeating.

The most expensive coffee in the world costs $100 per cup and $600 per pound. Why does it cost so much? In West Java, Indonesia, the colonial coffee growers exploited the native coffee bean pickers. They would not allow them to drink coffee from the valuable coffee beans they picked. In the words of Scripture, they muzzled the ox that treaded the grain (Deuteronomy 25:4, 1

Timothy 5:18). The workers, however, did want to drink coffee. They knew that a certain mammal, the weird-looking civet cat, likes to eat the raw coffee beans. Those beans passed through the digestive system of the civet cat and came out in civet cat crap. The local workers picked the beans out of the dung, washed them, ground them, and made coffee from those beans. The growers grew curious about the workers' love of coffee from civet cat excrement. They tasted it. They found the power of poop.

It was the best coffee anyone had ever tasted. They marveled at the flavor, aroma, and taste of the civet cat crap coffee. It was supernaturally good. It just had a very strange origin. It turns out that there are enzymes in the digestive system of the civet cat that bathe the coffee beans with something that make the best coffee in the world. That is why you pay $100 a cup for the rare coffee. It went through a whole lot of dung to taste the way it tastes.

The Apostle Paul went through the same stuff. He reminds us in 2 Corinthians 11 that he was beaten with rods, whipped with whips, shipwrecked three times, hounded by robbers, and mistreated by the very churches he founded. Yet in 2 Corinthians 4:17, he exclaims, "This light momentary tribulation is working out an eternal weight of glory beyond all comparison." In the strangest way, God takes the worst situations and by a process only He understands, those very situations become the thing that leads to a life of glory beyond comprehension.

He can take a failed business and teach you how to be an entrepreneur next time.

He can take a betrayed marriage and teach you how to repair

what you thought was broken forever.

He can take a serious illness and turn you into a person of prayer and faith.

He can take a lonely, isolated, abandoned time and turn it into a time of spiritual formation.

What the digestive system of a civet cat can do for coffee, God can do in the strangest ways through the difficult situations you confront. The Bible does not explain how He does it, but it exclaims that He does do it. Out of the worst situations can come life with a new flavor and texture better than anything before.

You can praise God for that. In the Old Testament book of Nehemiah, the Jewish layman led the discouraged Jews to rebuild the wall of Jerusalem that rested in ruins. After they rebuilt the wall, he divided the Hebrew choir into two groups. They marched clockwise and counterclockwise around the wall singing the praises of God. They sang at the Temple gate, the sheep gate, and the water gate. That was easy to do. Who would not want to sing at the gate by the Temple, or the gate where the sacrificial sheep came into the city, or the gate by the water supply in that arid land?

But the text also tells you that they stopped and sang praises at the dung gate. That gate was at the far south end of the wall, distant for obvious reasons. Yet they stopped and sang praises to God at the least likely of all gates, the dung gate. That is where the excrement from thousands of animals was carried out of the city. Camels, donkeys, goats, sheep, and horses all made the streets filthy. There was a mountain of dung at the dung gate. Yet they praised God at the dung gate. There is power in praise at the poop of life.

Life will hand you difficult situations in hard places. You will have to praise God, if you praise Him at all, sometimes at the dung gate. After all, God took the worst thing ever done on earth and used it for salvation. That was the crucifixion of His own Son. Yet God used that to save the world and to be the foundation of our faith.

PAUSE TO PONDER
II Corinthians 11:22-31

"Are they Hebrews? So am I. Are they Israelites? So am I. Are they descendants of Abraham? So am I. ²³ Are they servants of Christ?—I am speaking as if insane—I more so; in far more labors, in far more imprisonments, beaten times without number, often in danger of death. ²⁴ Five times I received from the Jews thirty-nine lashes. ²⁵ Three times I was beaten with rods, once I was stoned, three times I was shipwrecked, a night and a day I have spent adrift at sea. ²⁶ I have been on frequent journeys, in dangers from rivers, dangers from robbers, dangers from my countrymen, dangers from the Gentiles, dangers in the city, dangers in the wilderness, dangers at sea, dangers among false brothers; ²⁷ I have been in labor and hardship, through many sleepless nights, in hunger and thirst, often without food, in cold and exposure. ²⁸ Apart from such external things, there is the daily pressure on me of concern for all the churches. ²⁹ Who is weak without my being weak? Who is led into sin without my intense concern?

³⁰ If I have to boast, I will boast of what pertains to my weakness. ³¹ The God and Father of the Lord Jesus, He who is blessed forever, knows that I am not lying."

MONDAY

What are the things right now that you can identify as poop?
Maybe a co-worker, a neighbor, an errant relative or a situation
is poop. What are you going through? Will you give it to God?

TUESDAY

Think through the Bible and great Christians who faced poop.
Joseph was sold by his brothers, but he wound up the COO
of Egypt. Billy Graham was opposed by the liberals and the
fundamentalists when he began his epochal ministry.
Nobody remembers his opponents but the world has never
forgotten his impact.

WEDNESDAY

R. T. Kendall wrote about sanctifying the trial. Give the trial
to God. Hand it to him in prayer. Ask Him to do what only
He can do about it.

THURSDAY

Reflect on your own life and the way God in the past has
turned trials into triumphs.

FRIDAY

Encourage a friend who is going through trials with your own
past lessons and victories. It will confirm you in your faith.

ARE YOU A KEEPER?

My buddy Jim Phillips is a competitive bass fisherman and a preacher. He fishes for fish and men. He has some platinum level fishing stories. Like a lot of folks who breathe the clean air of the outdoors, Jim also has some deeper insights. Competitive fishermen are judged on a total catch of bass at the weigh-in at the end of the day. Some fish are marginal at the point of keeping them in the live well as a fish worthy of the competition. The fisherman must decide whether a marginal fish is a keeper or needs to be tossed back into the lake. From the fish's viewpoint, I expect none of them want to be a keeper. They would rather go back where they came from. There's nowhere like home, even for a fish. For the purposes of the competition, however, some are keepers, and some are not. Jim suggests some larger lessons for life and eternal life based on his experience. I have some ideas, too.

In our lives as men, we face a similar choice in most of life's significant decisions. For one, consider your marriage. In the will of God, a Christian man must consider, before taking vows, whether or not the woman he is marrying will be a keeper. That does not mean if she looks like Beyoncé (or for my generation Pamela Anderson or Farah Fawcett). A lot of women look good before you get them into the boat, only to find out you have caught the wrong lady and she just might sink your ship. Some of my friends had a wife that was a keeper but they did not keep her. They have lived to regret that. Even if you are on round two or three of the marriage merry-go-round, at each turn you need to seriously ask if this lady is a keeper in the will of God before you jump in the boat.

You need to decide if you will treat your kids as keepers. I don't mean you will throw them back into the lake. I do mean that you have a lifelong obligation to those kids. You must always treat them like keepers. There is no sending them back. Your influence in their lives is indispensable. No teacher, pastor, or social worker can ever take your place.

When I sit with dying men, the main thing they talk about is their family. Not one of them ever told me with his last breath, "I wish I had done one more deal." Many of them have told me, "I would give anything to go back and spend more time with my family."

You can do that, regardless of the age of your kids. One of the healthiest things about millennials is their absolute intention to stay in touch with their families. Unfortunately, for many in my generation, we were out of there when we were adults. The current generation wants to be keepers.

You need to decide if your career is a keeper. Most men have several careers in this season of history. Even retirees are going back to work in record numbers, not because they must but because they want to. As a famous commercial once said, "You only go around once in life." They tried to get you to drink their beer, as if that is what life is about. The slogan is true, but the beverage is a silly answer to the profound statement. You should weigh where you will spend the eight-plus hours a day at work. Is that the vocation that God has for you?

Most significantly, when you come to the end and meet God, will He consider YOU a keeper? None of us, not one, is born a keeper. We have all sinned and fallen short of His expectations. Our most righteous acts are like the worst shop rag on the floor. Out best moment is so tainted with ego that we are all spiritual narcissists. We are not born keepers. The only way you can be a keeper at the end is to be born again. You were born physically not a keeper. Yet you can be born again as a keeper. Nicodemus came to Jesus by night. I call him "Nick at Night." He thought he was a keeper. Jesus told Nick that he had to be born again to be a keeper.

At the final judgment you want to be a keeper. You want the living God and the Lord Jesus Christ to keep you with all the saints of the ages gathered around the throne of God. What an awful thing for the Son of God, who died for you, was buried for you, and rose from the dead for you, to tell you at the end, "You are not a keeper. I lived a perfect life for you. I opened my veins and died a horrible death for you. I rose for you, but you told me that did not matter to you. Depart from me."

That is a scene you do not want to be in. You do not have to be in that picture. The Apostle Paul famously said, "For me to live is Christ and to die is gain" (Philippians 1:21). You can be a keeper for Christ.

Here is where the comparison with a fish ends. Fish who are keepers are doomed. Their destiny is the frying pan. They are a keeper for only a short time. They had a reprieve when they were thrown into the live well, but that is short-lived. A fish does not want to be a keeper, but you do.

Have you settled this matter of personal salvation in your life once-and-for-all? You may not be sure. You may be vague about it. You may be nervous about it. But you can be sure about it. Just confess to Him that you know you are not born a keeper. Tell Him that your only hope is for Him to keep you. Tell Him you do not have a ghost of a chance unless He receives you as His own. Receive Him just as you would receive me if I showed up on your front porch and rang the bell. Invite Jesus into your life. Do not worry about how you say it; just mean it. If you ever once confess that Jesus is Lord and believe that God raised Him from the dead, you are a keeper (Romans 10:8-10). The deal is sealed. Heaven is your destination. You do not know your ETA, but you know you will land there.

"But what does it say? "The word is near you, in your mouth and in your heart"—that is, the word of faith which we are preaching, [9] that if you confess with your mouth Jesus as Lord, and believe in your heart that God raised Him from the dead, you will be saved; [10] for with the heart a person believes, resulting in righteousness, and with the mouth he confesses, resulting in salvation. [11] For the Scripture says, "Whoever believes in Him will not be put to shame." [12] For there is no distinction between Jew and Greek; for the same Lord is Lord of all, abounding in riches for all who call on Him; [13] for "Everyone who calls on the name of the Lord will be saved."

MONDAY

Remember the time and place you committed your life to Christ, and He became your Savior. It may have been a crisis followed by a process, but you need some memory of it.

TUESDAY

Who are the keepers in your own life? Who do you need to keep regardless? Stop and think.

WEDNESDAY

What in your life right now would keep you from having the testimony and influence you know the Lord wants you to have? If you want to be a keeper, you must let some things go.

THURSDAY

Creatively imagine that moment to come when you stand before the Lord Jesus Christ (2 Corinthians 5:10). What will that appointment be like? You will want to be a keeper.

FRIDAY

Identify someone you know who is losing his footing in the Christian life, being tested and tried at this time. Encourage them to persevere, stand their ground, and pray their way through.

COMPOSURE

"My self is a thing that I must now compose...as one composes a speech. What I must present is a 'made' thing. Not something born."
—MARGARET ATWOOD, THE HANDMAID'S TALE

Remaining composed belongs to what most thinking persons desire. Not to be shaken, never to be overreactive, always to be poised, is the goal for most mature people. Most of your friends who fly off at the handle never make a good landing. Atwood supposes you can compose yourself in the same way you compose a speech. That is an ideal, but it is seldom achievable. We need some "self beyond ourselves" if we are to stay composed. We cannot make ourselves composed but there is One Who can compose us.

Jesus never demonstrated a loss of composure. Tempted, belittled, opposed, the object of treachery and finally the recipient of a beating, a cross, and painful death, He remained composed throughout. On Tuesday of Holy Week, just three days before

His Cross, he was confronted by every level of religious leader in His time, all of them attempting to best Him in public debate. The fundamentalist Pharisees, the liberal Sadducees, the political Herodians, and the flotsam and jetsam of the crowd all tested Him in public. He remained perfectly composed. At the end of that trying day Jesus told his apprentices, "You know that after two days is Passover, and the Son of Man will be delivered up to be crucified" (Matthew 26:2).

Consider the composure of that statement. Having been involved in controversy all day, He speaks with a supernatural composure. He indicates His painful and humiliating death just two days away, as if it were an appointment on his calendar, not a tormenting tragedy. Then he leaves to go to a banquet.

At the banquet, Jesus makes a similarly composed remark after a woman anoints Him with oil: "For in pouring this fragrant oil on My body, she did it for my burial" (Matthew 26:12).

Consider how rare that would be today. What if you were at the table with a friend and an undertaker. Suddenly, the undertaker pours some formaldehyde on your friend. Rather than object, what if your friend simply said, "He's just getting ready to bury me in a couple of days." That shock would shake the occasion. Yet when Jesus was being publicly embalmed two days before His Cross, he spoke with a mature certainty of His crucifixion two days hence. The Passover and Lord's Supper would become like a prisoner's last meal. When He investigated the red wine, He saw His own blood. When he ripped apart the Passover bread, He saw His flesh ripped from His bones. Yet in all of this you see the composed Christ. In the coming torchlight parade and kangaroo court, everyone else hurries and presses; He stands in supreme composure above all this zoo of human anger and revenge.

When Jesus is on trial before Pilate, He is more the judge than His judge. Dying in pain, He deliberately opens the door to heaven for a convict dying beside him. How can we demonstrate that same composure?

Only in fellowship with Him can we demonstrate His composure. You cannot compose yourself; it is beyond human willpower. You will lose it. You will explode at those closest to you unless you live in constant contact with Christ the composer. You do not compose yourself by looking within. You do not compose yourself by meditating or saying some sacred mantra ten thousand times. You stay composed only by looking outside yourself at Christ the composer. In meditating on Him, giving every situation to Him, and living in constant contact with Him, you find yourself composed.

Fifty years after Dietrich Bonhoeffer was executed, the Nazi doctor who pronounced him dead was still wondering at his composure. The 39-year-old Lutheran pastor stood on the scaffold to be hanged, and with complete calm said, "This is for me the end – the beginning of life." That April 9, 1945, witnessed a perfectly composed young man interpret his own death as the beginning of life. He did not start to live that way on the scaffold. He had lived with the same Christ daily in a striking way. The composure of the Christ became his composure. It can be yours as well.

PAUSE TO PONDER
MATTHEW 26:26-35

"Now while they were eating, Jesus took some bread, and after a blessing, He broke it and gave it to the disciples, and said, "Take, eat; this is My body." 27 And when He had taken a cup and given thanks, He gave it to them, saying, "Drink from it, all of you; 28 for this is My blood of the covenant, which

is being poured out for many for forgiveness of sins. 29 But I say to you, I will not drink of this fruit of the vine from now on until that day when I drink it with you, new, in My Father's kingdom."

30 And after singing a hymn, they went out to the Mount of Olives.

31 Then Jesus said to them, "You will all fall away because of Me this night, for it is written: 'I will strike the shepherd, and the sheep of the flock will be scattered.' 32 But after I have been raised, I will go ahead of you to Galilee." 33 But Peter replied to Him, "Even if they all fall away because of You, I will never fall away!"34 Jesus said to him, "Truly I say to you that this very night, before a rooster crows, you will deny Me three times." 35 Peter said to Him, "Even if I have to die with You, I will not deny You!" All the disciples said the same thing as well."

MONDAY

Recall the last time you "lost it." You blew your top. You overreacted. You embarrassed your own Christian testimony in front of someone working with you. Reflect on that. Lean back into it. Feel the bitterness of it. Then, give it to Christ. Hand it to Him.

TUESDAY

Consider those persons who are always trying to test your composure. Who are they? What are the situations? Imagine Jesus in front of you right now. Give those people to Him. Call their names and hand them to Him.

WEDNESDAY

Meditate today on the composure of Christ. Read any chapter from the four Gospels. Ask yourself how He demonstrated His composure.

THURSDAY

Ask Christ to live His life through you at the point of composure. Confess that you cannot, but He can. Ask Him to take your life, like an empty glove, and fill it with His calm hand.

FRIDAY

Share this secret with someone you know who struggles with composure.

CHAPTER 14

ROPED TOGETHER

Alpine climbers use a definite system for protection as they go for the peak. They tether themselves together, usually about 30 feet apart. The climber at the top of the climbers anchors himself with an ice pick and piton deeply buried into the ice or snow. That piton is the lifeline for all climbers below if one of them slips and dangles helplessly in the mid-air. The climber who falls free from the face of the mountain depends on the climber highest above for an anchor point. The same kind of thing is done by rock climbers in Yosemite and elsewhere.

The climbers further down may be so far from the climber on the top that they can only trust that the climber at the top of the group has a strong anchor. They are dependent on someone above that they cannot see.

As believers in Christ, you and I are in the same situation. We have bet our very eternal lives on Someone above that we cannot see. He anchors our lives. As we come and go, drive and fly, sleep and wake, encounter illness and death, we depend on the One above Who is our anchor. We are roped together with Him.

At the very top of that rope, closest to Him, are the apostles and eyewitnesses of His life on earth. Peter, John, Paul and the others are closest to Him, in the eternal world above. After them come the saints of every century. They all testify to us that the anchor holds. You and I are the believers at the very bottom of the rope. We have the testimony of millions before us that the anchor holds. Yet we do not see the Lord at the top of the rope. He has ascended into the heavens above.

In the dark days of World War II, Ruth Caye Jones was the wife of a pastor and mother of five children. During perilous and threatening times, she took a notepad out of her apron, and with a pencil wrote the words and music of a beloved song:

In times like these, you need a Savior.
In times like these, you need an anchor;
Be very sure, be very sure,
Your anchor holds and grips the Solid Rock!
This Rock is Jesus, Yes, He's the One.
This Rock is Jesus, the only One.
Be very sure, be very sure,
Your anchor holds and grips the Solid Rock!

Ruth lived to see George Beverly Shea sing her song with the mass choirs at the Billy Graham crusades. She wept when she thought of the years before when she wrote those words on a little notepad.

Enormous significance rests with the words of that song. You may be depending on your health; it can disappear in a moment. You could trust your savings; ask the people in Venezuela about hyperinflation. You could be anchored in your network; friends can and do disappear in bad times.

Never before in my life have I experienced the consequences of a Pandemic: sheltering in place, essential and non-essential workers, social distancing and the like. For me and many others, this pandemic has meant separation from loved ones, lost income, depression, and fear of the unknown. And when we felt like our moorings were coming loose, we found that nothing on this planet can anchor you like Jesus.

Spend the days this week handing to Him everything you depend on and confess that there is no anchor but Him.

PAUSE TO PONDER
Hebrews 6 :19-20

"This hope we have as an anchor of the soul, a hope

both sure and reliable and one which enters within

the veil, [20] *where Jesus has entered as a forerunner*

for us, having become a high priest forever according

to the order of Melchizedek."

MONDAY

Confess that your business could disappear. Put it into his hands. "Lord, anchor my business."

TUESDAY

Put your health into His hands. Acknowledge that your health is fragile and that you depend on Him. "Lord, anchor my health."

WEDNESDAY

Put your network and friends into His hands. Acknowledge that in a catastrophe you could all be in the same trouble. "Lord, I put all my friends in your hands."

THURSDAY

Put your family into His hands. Even though it is unthinkable, families do sometimes break apart in the strangest ways. Put your fragile family into His hands. "Lord, take my family into your hands."

FRIDAY

Put your wealth into His hands. Another 1929, 2008, or 2020 could change everything for all of us. We have found out that everything material is fragile. "Lord, I put my wealth into your hands. Give me not what I want but what I need."

YOUR SIN IS BIGGER
THAN MINE

An older religion professor at my alma mater taught introductory New Testament to 18-year-old freshmen. Sometimes these newly minted high school graduates asked him unnerving questions. As he taught the Sermon on the Mount, he explained Jesus' famed statement, "Whosoever looks on a woman to lust after her has committed adultery already in his heart." A bright-eyed freshman woman asked him, "Does that mean adultery in the head is as bad as adultery in the bed?" Unsettled, he explained that all sin is the same before God but not all sin has the same consequences. Adultery in the head affects you. Adultery in the bed involves three other people: your spouse, the partner in adultery, and the other spouse.

We do like to rank sins, do we not? A friend said Pentecostals have a long list of sins, Baptists a shorter list, and Episcopalians hardly have a list at all. An Episcopal priest told a friend of mine that he had to have a drink in his hand or otherwise his members thought he was an alcoholic.

The story is told of an old Pentecostal woman coming up to young Billy Graham in a hotel lobby and demanding to know what he thought about women wearing makeup. Graham told her, "I think some would do you good." We get in some odd situations by ranking sins. The ice-tea-drinking Baptist deacon who put on a sheet and terrorized black folks considered his sin much less than the martini drinking Catholic next door. We all play that game.

The most common sin game is "your sin is bigger than my sin, so I feel better about myself." The man with a volcanic temper feels better about himself because he never really beat his wife. The beautiful, vain woman feels better about her vanity because she never was divorced. The liar feels better than the thief who gets caught. And on and on and on. For uncounted millions, self-esteem is propped up because they can find a bigger sinner than their own. They puff up their own worth by demoting someone else. They can live a life singing off key because someone else can't sing a note.

No wonder my Mom told me as I left for college, "Promise me you won't do the big sins." I was a new believer and I said, "But Mom, sin is sin." She said, "I know, but don't do the BIG ONES!"

We all misunderstand the nature of a holy God. The slightest sin affronts the holiness of God. When a great musician hears a note off key it gives him a pain that the novice cannot understand. When a great poet hears a garbled mumbo-jumbo of terrible rhymes it gives him a discomfort the unpoetic hack cannot understand. When someone who can shoot an entire box of clays at a range watches a beginner who cannot hit one, it gives him a sense of pity for such a poor shot. When a par golfer watches a beginner at the driving range toe a ball and hit the man at the next tee, it gives him a revulsion that the hacker cannot comprehend.

These awkward comparisons do not touch the pain of a holy God at the slightest hint of impurity. To compare human sins in His presence is like comparing two molehills to Mount Everest, two thimblefuls of water to the Pacific Ocean, or two galaxies to a single atom in space. There is no comparison. The attempt is absurd. The difference in perspective between this sin and that sin compared to the holiness of God is so small as to be ridiculous. For me to be proud that I have not killed somebody compared with someone who has killed somebody shrinks into nothingness when my anger is compared to someone else's homicide in the presence of a Holy God.

We try to puff ourselves up because we do not understand this. The most righteous moment of our lives is so shot through with ego as to be worthy of eternal commendation by a Holy God. We humans are a contradiction. A bear acts like a bear and nobody blames him. A dog acts like a dog and nobody blames him. We do not condemn a vulture for eating a vulture diet.

Yet we humans live in a total contradiction. Made in the image of God, we have all written graffiti over that image. We are walking, talking, breathing contradictions. That is why comparing your sin to my sin is ridiculous. Apart from the rich, undeserved pardoning mercy of God, we are all in hell. That is, there can be conversions when someone has one foot in life and another one slipping into the grave. You cannot mix merit and mercy. God either demands equal merit or He gives equal mercy.

Thank God there is a wideness of mercy and there is a kindness in His justice that is more than we can imagine. Stop the comparison game. Some sins are Peoria and some sins are Chicago, but they are all in the same state.

PAUSE TO PONDER
ROMANS 3 :21-26

"But now apart from the Law the righteousness of God has been revealed, being witnessed by the Law and the Prophets, 22 but it is the righteousness of God through faith in Jesus Christ for all those who believe; for there is no distinction, 23 for all have sinned and fall short of the glory of God, 24 being justified as a gift by His grace through the redemption which is in Christ Jesus, 25 whom God displayed publicly as a propitiation in His blood through faith. This was to demonstrate His righteousness, because in God's merciful restraint He let the sins previously committed go unpunished; 26 for the demonstration, that is, of His righteousness at the present time, so that He would be just and the justifier of the one who has faith in Jesus."

MONDAY

Inventory your own sins, known and unknown, in comparison with the sins of those in your closest circle. Do you ever feel smug about your sins? Be honest. Sit and soak in it.

TUESDAY

What damage have you seen done to others when sins are compared? Who is really helped or redeemed by the comparison of sins? Audit your experience of seeing this.

WEDNESDAY

Today practice knowing the depth of your own sins all day long and see what it does to your attitude to the person at the counter of the dry cleaners, the waitress who spills the soup, or the colleague who misses a deadline.

THURSDAY

Find someone you know has committed visible sins that you have not committed. Prop that person up with friendship, mercy, and solidarity.

FRIDAY

Look at the Cross. See Jesus covered with your anger, deceit, impatience, jealousy, and hidden thoughts. See Him bleeding, dying, and looking at you. Does that change your attitude about the sins of others?

RIGHT PERSON: WRONG PLACE

Without question Lamar Jackson has stunned the NFL world. The Baltimore whiz cannot be explained in normal football terms. Yet Hall of Fame General Manager Bill Polian, who said Lamar should convert to wide receiver, has admitted he was wrong: "I used the old, traditional quarterback standard…bottom line, I was wrong."

A revered football expert wanted to put the right man in the wrong place. As in football, so also in life. You yourself may have been forced into the wrong place by your own decisions, the decisions of others, or the stuff that happens in life. One of the great preachers in the English language, G. Campbell Morgan, was told he could not preach and should be a schoolteacher. It happens. What can we learn from this?

The Apostle Paul compared the church to a human body (1 Corinthians 12:12-26). The church functions when each member takes the place that God has sovereignly appointed for that member. The hand cannot discount the foot. The eye cannot belittle the ear. The analogy is obvious. In the great plan of God each of you has his own place. Find that place, embrace it, and lean into it. This is what gives life its fulfillment.

Sometimes men force themselves into the wrong place. One of the stupidest current statements is the unqualified advice, "Find your passion and do that." Even Bill Gates has called that ridiculous. What if your passion is growing radishes? For you, life looks like one big radish. To plant them, smell them, cook with them, and eat them is your consuming passion. Well, get a clue. There is no future for you in devoting your life to radishes. Hitler followed his passion and so did Stalin. See how that worked. Wisdom (James 1:5) is finding where God wants you and planting your feet there.

Other times someone else puts a man in the wrong place. A parent decides you must go to college even though your skills are bent toward fixing things. A teacher pushes you down a path in which you have no interest. A spouse nags you into a career that fits like a bad pair of shorts. A whole bunch of people all say you must do "x" when you know you are cut out to do "y". Sometimes you need to tell everyone that life is not a dress rehearsal. This is the only one you have on this planet.

There are times you just wind up in the wrong place and you do not know how you got there. Joseph found himself a slave, because he would not have sex with his boss's wife he went to jail, and the one person who could have helped him forgot about him for two years. Circumstances put him in the wrong place, but ended up being a step towards the right place.

The best news of Jesus Christ is this: God can start with you wherever you are, and things will be better for you than they could ever have been otherwise. Now notice what I did not say. I did not say that bad choices have no consequences. They do. I did not say you get to go back and take a mulligan on every bad decision you ever made. You cannot. What I did say is this: you can start with God right now and things will be better than they could ever have been any other way. He can start where you are regardless of how you got there. It will be better than it could have been any other way.

The ultimate picture of the wrong man in the right place is the cross. There Jesus, who did not deserve the cross, took my place so I do not face the consequences of rebellion against God. He was the wrong man, however, on the cross. It should have been me and it would have been me except for the mercy of God displayed on that cross.

PAUSE TO PONDER
I Corinthians 12 :12-26

*"For just as the body is one and yet has many parts, and
all the parts of the body, though they are many, are one body,
so also is Christ.* [13] *For by one Spirit we were all baptized into
one body, whether Jews or Greeks, whether slaves or free,
and we were all made to drink of one Spirit.*

[14] *For the body is not one part, but many.* [15] *If the foot says,
"Because I am not a hand, I am not a part of the body," it is not
for this reason any less a part of the body.* [16] *And if the ear says,
"Because I am not an eye, I am not a part of the body," it is not for
this reason any less a part of the body.* [17] *If the whole body were an
eye, where would the hearing be? If the whole body were hearing,
where would the sense of smell be?* [18] *But now God has arranged the
parts, each one of them in the body, just as He desired.* [19] *If they were
all one part, where would the body be?* [20] *But now there are many
parts, but one body.* [21] *And the eye cannot say to the hand, "I have
no need of you"; or again, the head to the feet, "I have no need of
you."* [22] *On the contrary, it is much truer that the parts of the body
which seem to be weaker are necessary;* [23] *and those parts of the
body which we consider less honorable, on these we bestow greater
honor, and our less presentable parts become much more presentable,*
[24] *whereas our more presentable parts have no need of it. But God
has so composed the body, giving more abundant honor to that part
which lacked,* [25] *so that there may be no division in the body,
but that the parts may have the same care for one another.* [26]
*And if one part of the body suffers, all the parts suffer with
it; if a part is honored, all the parts rejoice with it."*

MONDAY

Ask God to give you a clear, personal revelation through his written word and shaped by your circumstances, about where you need to be.

TUESDAY

Find a spiritual partner that affirms God's leadership in your life. You cannot mix oil and water. A marriage with Christ is hard enough; a marriage without Him is virtually impossible.

WEDNESDAY

Get alone with God. Ask Him to search you and know you as He already does (Psalm 139). Plead with God to reveal His plan for your life to you so clearly that you cannot miss it. Sit. Wait.

THURSDAY

If God gave you an impression about the avenue of service you are to join, share this with you pastor.

FRIDAY

Get outside of yourself and find someone else struggling with the same questions. Partner up with him, make covenants to help one another in prayer, and stick by that person as you mutually share experiences in Christ.

CHAPTER 17

MORTALITY – NO EXCEPTIONS

Two times Mark Twain read his own obituary. The first time he was erroneously reported dead, he made his famous quip, "Rumors of my death are an exaggeration." The second false obituary claimed that he was lost at sea. After the second false, premature report of his death, he told of an adventure of being lost and recovered from the sea. Three years later he really did die.

William Saroyan once quipped, "I know everybody dies, but I thought an exception would be made in my case."

Unless Jesus does not end history by His visible, bodily return, you will die. As Tony Campolo said, "They will put you in a box, put the box in a box, put you in the ground, go back to the fellowship hall, eat potato salad, and talk about you."

Hebrews 9:27 just puts it out there, "And, as it is, it is appointed unto man to die, and after death the judgment." For centuries the principal duty of Christian preachers was to keep that before people. Dying ministers exhorted dying parishioners to get ready for death and judgment. People would dwell at length on their coming deathbed and eternity. Today, any preacher who did that with regularity would empty the pews. We want to know how to flourish now, as if forever does not exist.

Let me just cut it straight. You will die. There is either a God or there is not. If there is a God, the Bible either is His Word or it is not. IF the Bible is His Word, you will be consciously somewhere forever. You will either be with Christ in glory or a place so horrible we do not even like to think about it. Polls suggest that most Americans, 66% believe we survive somewhere after death. Even some agnostics believe the human spirit is so strong that it will survive somewhere.

Folks my age begin to think about mortality. A recent round of medical exams made me think about my own mortality. My Boomer friends are now checking out with regularity. The old folks who used to die are closer and closer to my age. Mentors are almost all gone. Peers are starting to go. How can we have the best attitude towards our own mortality? Theodore Roosevelt said, "Life and death are all part of the same great adventure."

First, deal with God about life and death. God sent His Son, Jesus. On the Cross Jesus tasted death for everyone. God took death into Himself on the Cross. God has tasted death in Christ. Part of dealing with God about death is the sting of sin. When death draws near, guilt, failure, and regret come marching in and standing around the deathbed. Christ forgives sin, forgets failure, but cannot erase regret. Regret does not go away. Like shrapnel embedded in flesh during the war, regret just keeps hurting. The best way to deal with regret is not to live a life that creates it.

Second, live your life knowing that it is a gift. When John Claypool's 10-year-old daughter Laura Lue died with leukemia, he had to come to grips with the awful loss. He worked out an understanding through his grief that all of life is a gift. Life is not an entitlement. We do not "deserve" life. We did not invent our existence. We did not make ourselves come into this world and we do not choose to leave it. What happens during our time here is a gift, every day of it.

G. K. Chesterton believed that every day God says to the sun, "Get up," and He also says to each of us, "Get up." This is not a naturalistic world with an absent God. God gives us every day. Life is a gift, not a possession.

Third, learn to recognize what the Irish folks call "thin places." There are places and times in our lives when the border between time and eternity, heaven and earth, is very thin. We need to sense those places. A hospice, a moment of personal insight, a picture of someone gone on to the other side, and we are standing at a thin place. Eternity seems to just be right there. Do not flee from thin places. Embrace the times when there seems to be a thin membrane between now and forever. Hang out there, feel it, and lean into it.

Fourth, think about your legacy. When Billy Graham died in 2018, the world paused to think of his legacy. Millions of people reflected on his life, preaching, and very personal influence in their own lives. It was a reminder to me that we all leave a legacy. You would do well to think about your legacy. When folks gather for your viewing, sit through your funeral, or visit your grave, what will they remember? You probably do not want them to think, "Regardless, Dad always stayed at the office late. Dad always fell into his chair exhausted at night and went to sleep. Dad ran off when we needed him." You want them to remember something better. Think of that soon and often.

PAUSE TO PONDER
JOHN 14 :1-6

"Do not let your heart be troubled; believe in God, believe also in Me. [2] In My Father's house are many rooms; if that were not so, I would have told you, because I am going there to prepare a place for you. [3] And if I go and prepare a place for you, I am coming again and will take you to Myself, so that where I am, there you also will be. [4] And you know the way where I am going." [5] Thomas said to Him, "Lord, we do not know where You are going; how do we know the way?" [6] Jesus said to him, "I am the way, and the truth, and the life; no one comes to the Father except through Me."

MONDAY

Reflect on those you have loved and lost. What do you remember? What does that mean to you?

TUESDAY

You are surrounded with reminders of mortality. Every ambulance, hospital, and pharmacy are among the reminders that you are mortal. Just today, take note of everything that reminds you of mortality.

WEDNESDAY

What would you change right now if you were in your casket and those closest to you were walking by, looking at your frozen features?

THURSDAY

Turn a corner and thank God for the gift of life. Thank him that you woke up this morning, could stand up and walk, could think and could go and do. Each one of those is a gift.

FRIDAY

Treat your loved ones today as if it were the last day you would ever see them. What would you say? What would you do?

CHAPTER 18

LEFTOVERS

Some food you want to eat right after it is cooked. For example, I don't know many men who like leftover hamburgers. When you cook a thick, juicy hamburger on a bun toasted just right with crisp lettuce, cold onions, and tomatoes sliced perfectly flat, you want that burger right now. Day old burgers are not popular. On the other hand, I like some things when they sit and soak. Collard greens, meatloaf, and pinto beans with a smoked turkey leg are all better when they vacation in the refrigerator overnight. Some mysterious chemical reaction causes collard greens, garlic, onions, salt, pepper, and a little bit of vinegar to be measurably better the second day. I am sure some culinary genius could tell me why, but I just like the mystery of it.

The days of our lives are somewhat like that. There are some moments that are to be savored in the moment for all they are worth. Looking at your new baby, the first walk through a new home, and graduation from school all belong to immediate consumption. You will enjoy looking at the pictures for years to come, but those kinds of moments belong to the present. You enjoy, celebrate, laugh, and live in the moment with some things.

On the other hand, life hands us some leftovers. Longtime friends, old places revisited, letters from years ago rediscovered, or an old collectible reappearing in the attic belong to life's delightful leftovers. I happened on my old Lionel model train engine a while back. Suddenly decades vanished and I am sitting under the Christmas tree running the wheels off of it from the moment I wake up until I fell asleep at the switch. Life's leftovers.

But life also gives us another kind of leftovers. I mean those things left over after something did not work out. Life after divorce leaves you with leftovers. So also does life after a job does not work out, a degree is not finished, a child is alienated, or a loved one goes on before us and we are left alone. An empty chair at the table on holidays, a vacation to a place you used to share with someone who no longer wishes to be there with you, or unfinished papers from an unfinished degree plan belong to life's leftovers. Unlike collard greens, those leftovers are difficult to digest. What do you do with the difficult leftovers?

Some men just stay stuck in the past. They cannot move on from divorce, grief, loss, or incompletion. They ponder, reflect, brood, and stick to the past like Gorilla glue. They will not let themselves let go. Last thing at night and first thing in the morning they are looking in the rearview mirror. Regrets, melancholy, and reliving past moments become their permanent agenda. They do nothing but walk backwards.

Other men act as if the past did not happen. They fill their lives with current activities, work, travel, and deadlines to suffocate the past. They have no leftovers because they push them to the back of the refrigerator and pretend they are not there. After a while, however, they start to stink, and the man must deal with them. Denial does not make leftovers go away.

How do you deal with life's indigestible leftovers in a godly way? First, you must admit that they are there. Denial is no solution. Hurt is hurt. Sad is sad. Loss is loss. If you cover them with foil and put them out of site, they will ultimately let you know they are there. The Christian life does not deny the reality of what is happening. Marx was wrong if he thought Christianity was the opiate of the people. Christian folks look reality right in the face. Dead means dead. Divorce means she is gone and not coming back. A lost job is just that, over. You lean into the loss, stare it straight in the face, and name it for what it is. When Jesus died on the Cross, they had to take His dead body down, get covered with the blood and gore, and face the fact He had died.

But the Christian does not stay stuck there. Once you have owned the leftover, it is time to disown the leftover as something that would end your life, discolor your days, and freeze you in the past. Paul told you to develop holy amnesia, "Forgetting those things that are behind..." When you have looked loss in the eye without blinking, it is time to turn around and press on. In the next breath Paul said, "Press on toward the high calling of God in Christ Jesus" (Philippians 3:12-14).

The disciples put Jesus in the tomb, but they did not leave Him there. When He rose from the dead, He did not tell them to go back to Calvary and live there the rest of their lives in regret. He pointed forward to the gift of the Spirit at Pentecost and His great commission to tell the whole world that He had risen. His command was not to look back but to go forward.

You have a limited number of days. The clock is ticking, and the calendar is turning. The longer you are on earth the faster time flies by. Every day stuck looking back is a day you will never recover. Salvation means you learn to live looking forward. Christ bought it. The Spirit taught it. Thank God my soul caught it. Press on!

PAUSE TO PONDER
JOHN 15 :26-27

"When the Helper comes, whom I will send to you from the Father, namely, the Spirit of truth who comes from the Father, He will testify about Me, [27] and you are testifying as well, because you have been with Me from the beginning."

MONDAY

Savor a good leftover from the past. Remember a cherished friendship. Look at something you collected or built with your own hands that reminds you of delight in the past. Take an inventory of life's good leftovers.

TUESDAY

Where are you stuck in the past? A relationship gone, a job lost, or a bad deal that went south? Identify places you are stuck and ask God how to get unstuck. Sit, think, turn off your cell phone, and reflect on what keeps you stuck in the past.

WEDNESDAY

Invent a ritual to let go of the past. One friend stopped on a bridge and threw rocks in a river. Each rock represented a leftover to dismiss. Make a real event of letting go. Write the hurtful leftovers on a piece of paper. Set it on fire and repeat the words of Paul, "Forgetting those things that are behind."

THURSDAY

Make a proactive move today to empower your future by making the first step into something wholesome, positive, and engaging. Look at a new hobby or find a possible rental property. Pick up a book or watch Ken Burns' documentaries on baseball or jazz or World War II. Decide to lose 25 pounds and go to the gym today and get a trainer. Just do it. Hello, Nike.

FRIDAY

Get outside of yourself and help someone else who is stuck. It helps you forget your own junk to help someone else have a mental garage sale to get rid of their junk. Stand by someone today who needs to get unstuck and gently suggest the first step they need to take to let go.

DETOX

Many of us focus on external cleansing. Dirt on your face, grease on your hands, or a spot on your blazer and you will get rid of it immediately. External cleansing is obvious. You can see the need for it and others can see it. You have an immediate motivation to get rid of the stain or blemish. Fortunately for most of us, our inward need for cleansing is not obvious.

At the center of the internal detox system is the liver, but the heart, lungs, and kidneys also play a part. Your body manufactures millions of molecules daily in order to detox your system physically. You are a walking detox machine and you do not even know that it is happening. Awake and asleep, you are detoxing.

Folks needing additional detox from alcohol or other drugs may do it at a clinic, a luxury detox center, or at home with guidance and prescriptions. Physical detox takes time, medication, sometimes hurts, and has symptoms. Detox may take from a month to a year. Sometimes people must take Xanax or another anti-anxiety drug.

Detox may create pain, restlessness, and cramps. Confusion, anxiety, seizures, and agitation may accompany detox. It is not a pleasant experience at the beginning, but the outcome is more than worth it.

Spiritual detox has striking similarities to physical detox. Just like physical detox, you must come to a point of admitting that you need it. Sometimes others confront you with that crying need. You must own yourself before you can disown yourself. We all live in denial about something. The first step to spiritual detox is the admission that I need it right now.

Like physical detox, spiritual detox takes time. You did not get into the poisonous, toxic inward state of life overnight. Years of hurt, rejection, degradation, loss, and disruption poisoned you. You have done some things to yourself, and malicious people have done some things to you. That has created the internal poison that you need to detoxify. It did not happen overnight, and it will not go away overnight. Since Jesus took 40 days in the wilderness to focus on His coming work, it will take you at least that long. There is a reason Moses was on the mountain for 40 days, the church waiting in the Upper Room longer than that, and Paul was in the Arabian desert for three years. You will take time for spiritual detoxification.

You may literally need physical medicine for spiritual detox. Forget the stigma, don't worry about the gossips, visit a psychiatrist if necessary and get what you need to survive radical change in your life. Luke the physician worked with Paul. There are two interesting words for their work. The Greek word for what Luke did gives us our English word therapy. The word for what Paul did suggests miraculous spiritual healing. It took them both to do it.

Spiritual detox hurts. You must confront the garbage in you and the people you have hurt around you. It is not always easy to look at the man in the mirror. When I was a kid, I would get splinters in my fingers. My mom would heat up a sewing needle to sterilize it and then go after the splinter with needle and tweezers. I still remember how scared I was and how much it hurt. 99.9% of me was just fine, did not hurt, and had nothing to do with the splinter. Yet when mom worked on my splinter it made me hurt all over. All my focus was on that tiny place that hurt. Spiritual detox is like that. The deep inner hurt may be at one point in your life – marriage, loss, or rejection at work. Yet you hurt all over while you deal with it.

The good news from the Gospel is just this: The Lord is the great detoxifier. Read Psalm 51. Ponder 1 John 1:9. Consider James 4:4. Let God be as good as God really is. He is the cleansing, healing, restoring God. The moment you take a step towards Him He has already taken a step toward you. God is for you, with you, in you, behind you, protecting you from the past and in the front of you making a way to the future. Moses needed detox from anger, David from adultery and murder, Peter from denial, and Martha from too much busyness. The Bible is filled with heroes who needed detox. Get in line. You are next. We are all recovering from something.

PAUSE TO PONDER
PSALMS 51 :1-13

"Be gracious to me, God, according to Your faithfulness;
According to the greatness of Your compassion,
wipe out my wrongdoings.
2 Wash me thoroughly from my guilt
And cleanse me from my sin.
3 For I know my wrongdoings,
And my sin is constantly before me.
4 Against You, You only, I have sinned
And done what is evil in Your sight,
So that You are justified when You speak
And blameless when You judge.
5 Behold, I was brought forth in guilt,
And in sin my mother conceived me.
6 Behold, You desire truth in the innermost being,
And in secret You will make wisdom known to me.
7 Purify me with hyssop, and I will be clean;
Cleanse me, and I will be whiter than snow.
8 Let me hear joy and gladness,
Let the bones You have broken rejoice.
9 Hide Your face from my sins
And wipe out all my guilty deeds.
10 Create in me a clean heart, God,
And renew a steadfast spirit within me.
11 Do not cast me away from Your presence,
And do not take Your Holy Spirit from me.
12 Restore to me the joy of Your salvation,
And sustain me with a willing spirit.
13 Then I will teach wrongdoers Your ways,
And sinners will be converted to You."

MONDAY

Discover and admit today that you need detox at a specific spiritual place. Face it. Own it. Do not run from it. Give it a name: lust, greed, anger, prejudice…call it what it is.

TUESDAY

Set aside a definite time and place you will work on the detoxification. Perhaps a corner of your house at 7 a.m. each morning for a month to deal with it. Use web resources, books, Scripture, meditation and quietness to deal with it.

WEDNESDAY

Get an accountability partner to be sure you stay with it. Your pastor, elder, deacon, senior saint, or someone who is steady and predictable that can ask you, "How is it going for you?"

THURSDAY

Face the pain of the process. Like a marathon runner, press on through the pain of confrontation. Like peeling an onion, you will find new layers of detox. That's ok, God gave us tears to allow cleansing.

FRIDAY

Give yourself a break for a day. Breathe, walk, run, hunt, fish, collect something or just watch a mindless TV show. Detox takes time and you need a break.

CHAPTER 20

YOU CAN'T MAKE OLD FRIENDS

I am a Baylor Bear through and through. The greatest of all Baylor football games took place on a chilly November day in 1974. The Texas Longhorns, led by storied running back Earl Campbell, marched into Baylor Stadium as if they owned the place. There were more Texas fans than Baylor fans. At halftime the Bears looked doomed. Then the "Miracle on the Brazos" happened. Even though the BU line looked like toothpicks in comparison to the Horns and Earl Campbell dragged hapless BU tacklers down the field like wet rags, BU won. The quarterback, Neal Jeffrey, a tiny running back named Steve Beard and another runner named Phillip Kent beat the Horns 34-24 and sent shock waves through the football world. Young Grant Teaff became an overnight coaching sensation and the team won the SWC championship for the first time in five decades. Some 45 years later old Bears still ask, "Were you there?" "You bet, The Swan was there!"

What most do not know is the friendship of those team members with one another and with Coach Teaff has lasted to this very day.

On the 40th anniversary Coach Teaff had the entire team over to his house where with his gracious wife Donnell they celebrated again the day David beat Goliath. Running back Phillip Kent, who scored the last touchdown, keeps in touch with the coach and all the team members. They are friends for life.

You cannot make old friends. Forever friends must be cherished, written, called, and nurtured. When you get to a certain age you see more than ever the value of those who share heritage and memories with you. The loneliest of old folks are those who do not maintain and repair long-term friendships. It is more than worth the effort. Life's autumn and winter days will be warmed by conversations with old friends.

The opposite is also the case. You will regret the loss of friendships over things that are trivial. A friend recounted the story of two old Texas Baptist deacons who shared a common barbed wire fence. They had grown up together, raised their families together, built the same church together, and shared all of life on their ranches. Then one day a calf from one ranch got through the fence. They disagreed over who the calf belonged to. A half-century friendship was ruined over a calf. They sat in the same church and would not speak to one another. The entire community was shocked and saddened to see such a friendship ruined.

That must be the way the early Christians felt when they heard that Paul and Barnabas had a fight over John Mark. When they went on the first missionary journey Mark was fine and dandy if he was with Uncle Barnie on Cyprus. Everyone knew Uncle Barnie on Cyprus. But when they came to Turkey and the road was dangerous, Mark ran home to Jerusalem and mama. This caused a huge fight when Paul and Barnabas started to go on the second mission trip. Barnie wanted to take Mark. Paul said, "No." It split the dynamic duo for good. That must have saddened Peter and the rest of the disciples back home.

Take great care that old friendships are not ruined over politics or religion or prejudice or anything else. Old friends have too much in common to lose the friendship. Take the view "from the back of the hearse." When an old friend goes, you want to be able to know that your friendship lasted all the way. This old world can be cruel, lonely, and sometimes at the end, isolating. You will wish you kept friendships in repair. Do something right now to make certain that is the case.

PAUSE TO PONDER
JOHN 15 :12-17

"This is My commandment, that you love one another, just as I have loved you. [13] Greater love has no one than this, that a person will lay down his life for his friends. [14] You are My friends if you do what I command you.[15] No longer do I call you slaves, for the slave does not know what his master is doing; but I have called you friends, because all things that I have heard from My Father I have made known to you. [16] You did not choose Me but I chose you, and appointed you that you would go and bear fruit, and that your fruit would remain, so that whatever you ask of the Father in My name He may give to you. [17] This I command you, that you love one another."

MONDAY

Identify old friends. Make a list. Look through yearbooks,
Facebook, or old pictures. Don't procrastinate.

TUESDAY

Repair old friendships that got damaged. When you step out
into eternity you will be pleased with your last breaths that
you made peace with everyone. You cannot make alienated
friends like you but you can try to repair friendships.

WEDNESDAY

Make the next seven days "Contact a Friend Week." Each day
call, write, email, or visit an old friend. Get in the habit of
doing so.

THURSDAY

Find an old friend who has isolated himself. Urge that friend
to do the same. You will help them more than you know.

FRIDAY

Try to turn new friends into old friends. Not everyone can be
a long-term friend. Some folks are in your life for a season.
But try to make one new-old friend every year. You will be
bolstered up yourself and you will bless someone else.

A DRAMA QUEEN DISCIPLE

In 1989 Nolan Ryan struck out his 5000th batter. It is one sports record that will never be broken. Even though he never won the Cy Young Award, he is a legend of the game. One investigation concluded his fastball was the fastest in the storied history of the game. How did he keep on doing it? A little more than 20 minutes after his singular record, he was back down in the bowels of Arlington Stadium on an exercise bicycle. Nothing could keep him from his exercise routine. The moment of big drama was already a thing of the past. He faithfully returned to the little things that kept the big things going.

Christian discipleship is in some ways like that. Any number of us can imagine standing before a firing squad for Jesus. We can even think of bowing in the sand like the Arab Christians who have their heads chopped off for Jesus. Or we can imagine ourselves to be Chinese Christians whose churches are being burned for Jesus. The appeal of the dramatic is always with us. But most of life is not dramatic. Fred Craddock stated somewhere that he imagined he would write one big check for Jesus in a dramatic moment. Instead, the Christian life was 59 cents here, $1.09 there, and two bits somewhere else, and then life was done. For most Christians, faithful Christian living is far from dramatic. It is more like Nolan going back to his exercise bike day after day.

Peter provides a good example of that. Peter boldly proclaimed to Jesus, "Even if I have to die with You, I will not deny You!" (Matthew 26:35). Jesus warned him that would not be the case. What was the reality for Peter? He could not even stay awake during the most important prayer meeting in history. "Then He came to the disciples and found them sleeping, and said to Peter, 'What, could you not watch with me one hour?'" (Matthew 26:40). Just a mere 15 verses after claiming he would do the dramatic, Peter could not stay awake during a prayer meeting with Jesus.

Faithful Christian living is being true to Jesus in the humdrum, nitpicking, and sometimes mind-numbing details of everyday life. It means not barking back at a spouse when you are exhausted. It means listening to an employee explain the obvious to you when you have heard the same story hundreds of times. It means letting the person cut into line in front of you in traffic. It means buying a pair of socks for a bag lady at the drugstore who is pennies short of making the purchase. When we stand in front of Jesus it will be giving an account that we visited a sick person, went to see someone in prison, and gave an overcoat to a needy person.

The media has addicted us to the dramatic. I hate to say it, but 24/7 we are now bored with school shootings, California houses falling into mudslides, planes crashing, ships sinking, drugs killing people, and on and on in every news cycle. The dramas of life have seared our consciousness and left us wanting even more drama. Such life is like drinking saltwater. The more you drink the more you want to drink. That does not even account for those family members around us who thrive on creating constant dramas that would make the average opera look mundane. We all know persons who cannot live without the drama of the hour; they will invent one if none is around.

Amid all of this, Jesus calls you and me to a life of quiet, faithful discipleship. The late Dr. Jesse Fletcher said of piloting his own light single-engine aircraft, "It is hours and hours of boredom interrupted by a few moments of terror from time to time." Much of the Christian life is like that. You are not likely to be boiled in oil or have your feet frozen off in the tundra of Russia being a missionary. You are far more likely to spend part of life holding the hand of a dying spouse or propping up a wayward child or just being kind. And when you do, your life will fit another of Dr. Fletcher's great quotes – one I heard him say at Glorieta, New Mexico, at a college student conference in the mid 70's about missionary Bill Wallace in China: "He was an ordinary man but in the providence of God he lived an extraordinary life!" May that be a reality for you and me!

PAUSE TO PONDER
GALATIANS 2 :20

"I have been crucified with Christ; and it is no longer

I who live, but Christ lives in me; and the life which

I now live in the flesh I live by faith in the Son of God,

who loved me and gave Himself up for me."

MONDAY

Consider your own view of the daily Christian life. Are you waiting for the dramatic to serve Jesus? Does the tedious matter of quiet, faithful Christian living characterize your life rather than the big, loud, super, and dramatic?

TUESDAY

Identify today where you can serve Jesus in small, kind ways, even if people take advantage of you for doing so.

WEDNESDAY

The very best laboratory for the Christian life is your own home. Anyone can play like a good Christian on Sunday morning bellowing out hymns at church. What about the minute-by-minute life with your own spouse or kids?

THURSDAY

Reflect on the lives of the finest Christians around you. How do they demonstrate the life of Jesus in small ways?

FRIDAY

Start the day with a specific prayer that you will be sensitive even to tiny words and glances that show the presence of Christ in your life in mercy to others.

WHERE IS THE COMPASS?

There is an old joke around our house. From time to time, we committed the tomfoolery of going camping. I know that going out into the open under the stars building fires, roasting weenies and singing Kum-By-Yah is supposed to give great memories. That vision, however, does not count backing your car into a cow tank while turning around in a pasture, a rainstorm blowing down your tent, or various insects invading your pants. The old joke around our house, however, had nothing to do with that.

The old joke was, "Where is the compass?"

When we made our few camping trips, we always turned the house upside down looking for the compass. Was it with the tent, in the tool kit, with the tackle box, or at the bottom of some overstuffed desk drawer? We did not use the compass except on camping trips. We forgot the compass for months at a time. When we needed it, we had to search for it like Harrison Ford looking for the lost Ark. One thing always happened, however, when we found the AWOL compass: it always pointed north. We might lose the compass, but the compass never lost north. However deep it was buried in some dark closet, the compass still pointed north.

Sometimes we think we do not need a spiritual compass in life. We know where we want to go, what we want to get, and how we want to do it. With no direction, we live as if it were a moonless, starless night and we just go faster and faster in the fog with no direction. When all the roads run north and south, we decide to make our own way straight west, cutting across the clear roads that have always been there. Then we complain when we find swamps, deserts, rough places and nowhere comfortable to stay. We make our own way when there is already a way prepared for us. Then we complain that our way led to disaster.

Some men look at the Christian life as a burden, a hard row to hoe, or a straitjacket that confines them and ruins the fun in life. That is exactly the opposite of the case. The only people I know who experience any joy in this short life and difficult world are the people who use God's compass and get on God's road. If you think the Christian life is hard you ought to try sin and rebellion for a while. Cheat on your taxes and get caught by the IRS. Go to a massage parlor and wind up with your face on the front page of the local paper for giving money to an underage minor. Skim a little bit off your discretionary account at work and get exposed for embezzlement. Or just lie about where you are going one afternoon and get caught. Sin is hard. Sin does not work. You do not even have to have the Bible to prove that; just look around you. There is no stronger evidence of anything in the world than the single fact: sin does not work.

Just try to do the opposite of the Ten Commandments. Blaspheme, work seven days a week, kill, commit adultery, steal stuff, and covet everything you see. Find out if that really makes you happy. You are not the exception in human history. You do not break His commandments. They will break you.

God has given you a compass. You find it in His Ten Commandments, His Sermon on the Mount, and all the rest of His compasses. You will never keep its direction perfectly. The world, the flesh, and the devil will keep you from being perfect. Yet the fulfilling way of life is to pick up His compass when you drop it. It always points to true north in His world. You may have lost it. Find it today. His way is always the best way. It is also the way of joy, fulfillment, and meaning in life.

PAUSE TO PONDER
DEUTERONOMY 5 :1-21

"Now Moses summoned all Israel and said to them:

"Listen, Israel, to the statutes and ordinances which I am speaking today for you to hear, so that you may learn them and be careful to do them. 2 The Lord our God made a covenant with us at Horeb. 3 The Lord did not make this covenant with our fathers, but with us, all of us who are alive here today. 4 The Lord spoke with you face to face at the mountain from the midst of the fire, 5 while I was standing between the Lord and you at that time, to declare to you the word of the Lord; for you were afraid because of the fire, and you did not go up on the mountain. He said,

6 'I am the Lord your God who brought you out of the land of Egypt, out of the house of slavery.

7 'You shall have no other gods besides Me.

8 'You shall not make for yourself a carved image, or any likeness of what is in heaven above or on the earth beneath or in the water under the earth. 9 You shall not worship them nor serve them; for I, the Lord your God, am a jealous God, inflicting the punishment of the fathers on the children, even on the third and fourth generations of those who hate Me, 10 but showing favor to thousands, to those who love Me and keep My commandments."

11 'You shall not take the name of the Lord your God in vain,
for the Lord will not leave unpunished the one who takes
His name in vain.

12 'Keep the Sabbath day to treat it as holy, as the Lord your God commanded you. 13 For six days you shall labor and do all your work, 14 but the seventh day is a Sabbath of the Lord your God; you shall not do any work that day, you or your son or your daughter, or your male slave or your female slave, or your ox, your donkey, or any of your cattle, or your resident who stays with you, so that your male slave and your female slave may rest as well as you. 15 And you shall remember that you were a slave in the land of Egypt, and the Lord your God brought you out of there by a mighty hand and an outstretched arm; therefore the Lord your God commanded you to celebrate the Sabbath day.

16 'Honor your father and your mother, just as the Lord your God has commanded you, so that your days may be prolonged and that it may go well for you on the land which the Lord your God is giving you.

17 'You shall not murder.

18 'You shall not commit adultery.

19 'You shall not steal.

20 'You shall not give false testimony against your neighbor.

21 'You shall not covet your neighbor's wife, nor desire your neighbor's house, his field, his male slave or his female slave, his ox, his donkey, or anything that belongs to your neighbor.'

MONDAY

Take one of his commandments and commit yourself to remember it throughout the day. For example, take His commandment, "Do not covet." Spend the day without wanting other folks' stuff. Do not want someone else's car, house, wife, promotion, or appearance. Be satisfied with your clunker, thank God you have a roof over your head, enjoy your own wife, and stop worrying about your receding hairline.

TUESDAY

When you lose your way today, rebound. Don't spend the rest of the day feeling sorry for yourself that you screwed up. Tell God about it, ask His forgiveness, and find the compass.

WEDNESDAY

Where do you usually get off the mainline and on to the sideline? Where do you trade an aircraft carrier for a canoe? Where do you leave an eagle's nest and settle for a sparrow's nest? Put a name on the places you lose your compass and face the facts.

THURSDAY

Spend the day acknowledging to God that without His help you cannot go in the right direction. With the Lord, confess you cannot even find the right direction or locate the compass. Throw yourself on His mercy. Confess that without Him you cannot find your way.

FRIDAY

Get outside yourself and gently nudge your buddy in the right direction. This does not mean being holier than thou, interfering, or judgmental. It does mean to find a creative way to reorient someone around you who is about to get into a ditch.

THE COST OF DEMOLITION

When buildings must be torn down story by story, there is a steep demolition fee. The charge for destroying a building ranges from $4 to $8 per square foot. Typically, that means tearing the building down to the ground. It does not include hauling off the debris and may not include the cost of a license permitting the demolition, which may reach $10,000, as well as liability for other buildings. There is a high cost in demolishing buildings.

There is an even higher cost in demolishing people with words. Most native English speakers know between 20,000 and 30,000 words. Some studies suggest that the average adult uses about 7,000 words per day. How many of your words build up and how many tear down? The Apostle Paul had a thing to say about words that help and words that hurt:

Let no evil talk come out of your mouths, but only what is useful for building up, as there is need, so that your words may give grace to those who hear (EPHESIANS 4:29).

Paul is giving a list of character traits that reveal authentic Christians. One of them is a deliberate decision to use words that build up rather than tear down. Some litmus tests for the presence of Christian life are hard to trace: Is a person justified or sanctified or growing in general? This test is not that hard at all. Are you speaking words that build up or words that tear down? The Supreme Court in 1942 defined the term "fighting words":

Fighting words—those which by their very utterance inflict injury or tend to incite an immediate breach of the peace. It has been well observed that such utterances are no essential part of any exposition of ideas, and are of such slight social value as a step to truth that any benefit that may be derived from them is clearly outweighed by the social interest in order and morality.
— CHAPLINSKY V. NEW HAMPSHIRE, 1942

The case in question was about a cult member who cursed the town marshal who arrested him by calling him a cursed "racketeer" and "fascist." At the time those were fighting words. A friend of mine recalls his boyhood and what constituted fighting words. You could say almost anything except the words "yo mamma." Those were fighting words and led to bloody street fights. Most of us know in our culture, time, and place what are fighting words.

There are, however, other words that build people up. The Bible calls those words that "edify." That may seem like an odd, quaint, ancient word but it is at the heart of Christian speech. Christians are to use speech that builds up rather than words that tear down. Our country seems imprisoned in this season inside a prison of hateful words. The very next verse ties the use of hateful words to grieving the Holy Spirit, who is the very seal and guarantee of our redemption (4:30). The Holy Spirit is sensitive and hightails it out of your life when you use words that do not edify or build up.

Affirming words edify. Most people lack affirmation. Words spoken in childhood, school, work, military, or marriage have torn them down. Affirming words build up. They are words that validate who a person is and what a person does. Affirming words may be as simple as a quiet appropriate compliment about a person's appearance, performance, or presence. For example, virtually no one dislikes being told how young they look, how rested they look, or how smart they are.

Appreciative words edify. Most persons lack appreciation for their major contributions, and even less appreciation for minor things. In any marriage, office, or church it is almost impossible to be too appreciative. You do not have to save appreciation for someone who gives you a kidney. You can appreciate a tasty meal, a beautiful lawn, or a good job of carpentry. The opportunities for appreciation are as big as life.

Critical words do not edify. I have a friend who doubts there is such a thing as constructive criticism. Before you try that on someone, just recognize that for the most part that is what they hear most of the day. You really do not have to tell them that tie does not go with that suit or those flowers could be arranged better. Rest assured there are armies of people practicing "constructive criticism." Not one more instance of it is needed. If another guy's zipper is down and fly is open, obviously check your zipper so he can see it. If another guy's tie is not straight, work on straightening yours so he can see it. Try to be inventive in not using any kind of criticism. There was a skinny high school senior guy who took the largest girl in the class to the prom. He told her, "You sweat less than any big girl I ever danced with." That may not have been the most elegant way to say it, but his spirit was right. Of course, he had more work to do, but don't we all!

PAUSE TO PONDER
I Corinthians 10 :23-24

"All things are permitted, but not all things are of benefit.

All things are permitted, but not all things build people up.

24 No one is to seek his own advantage, but rather

that of his neighbor."

MONDAY

Ask yourself today before every statement you make to anybody
all day, "Does it edify?" If it does not, do not say it.

TUESDAY

Look for opportunities today to use speech that builds up:
Affirm, appreciate, adore.

WEDNESDAY

Read James 3 today concerning the power of the human tongue.
It can be a fire, a poison, and it can hurt like a runaway horse.

THURSDAY

Notice the people in your world who are encouragers.
Study their speech patterns when they speak and when
they are silent. Imitate them.

FRIDAY

Apologize to someone hurt by your speech. Suck it up and do it.
You will not regret it.

CHAPTER 24

TRADING GOLD FOR BRONZE

Today the value of bronze is 33 cents per ounce. The value of gold is $1,756.00 per ounce. If you are hedging your bet with precious metal, you would have to have 5,321 ounces of bronze in your safety deposit box to equal one ounce of gold. You might want to think about renting a storage space rather than a safety deposit box if you think the future is in bronze.

King Rehoboam was a jerk. His father was the wisest man in history, Solomon. When Solomon died, the wise old men counseled his arrogant son to take it easy on the kingdom. Ease in, keep taxes low, and keep a low profile. Instead, Rehoboam made a famous statement: "My little finger is thicker than my father's loins...my father disciplined you with whips, but I will discipline you with scorpions" (I Kings 12:10-11). As a result of his attitude and his idolatry, the son of the wisest man in history lost his kingdom.

Part of that loss was the loss of his father's famous gold shields.

When the invading Egyptians toppled the tinker toy throne of Rehoboam, he lost all Solomon's shields of gold. He replaced them with shields of bronze. Check the prices today for their relative worth. He inherited gold but his foolishness left him with bronze (1 Kings 11:26-27).

On Father's Day, we might well consider how much can change in a single generation. George Orwell said, "Every generation imagines itself to be more intelligent than the one that went before it, and wiser than the one that comes after it." This has always been the case. In the 4th century B.C., Aristotle said, "(young people) are high-minded because they have not yet been humbled by life, nor have they experienced the force of circumstances....They think they know everything, and are always quite sure about it." This view can be found in the literature from any age. Rehoboam, however, proved that such a view can lead to a downfall. We ought to consider several things about this:

One generation can exchange the gold of faith for the bronze of unbelief. The Christian faith is not automatically transmitted from one generation to the next. As I write this, the loss of millennials in the church is bemoaned everywhere, from Facebook posts to seminary leaders and more. A generation has opted out. There are as many explanations as there are pundits. The most faithful fathers cannot guarantee the transmission of faith to their children. Some devout fathers have produced hell-raisers and some hell-raisers have produced godly children.

You can see that in the very family of Rehoboam. His son Abijah was as sorry as Rehoboam, but his son Asa was godly. Go figure. What you can do is all you are able to do to rear your children with an example of living faith. You may say, "I have already blown that." You can start today, this very hour, to honor God and leave an example.

One generation can exchange the gold of discipline for the bronze of sloth. A work ethic in one generation may not produce the same in the next. A friend who has watched many car dealerships has traced a three-generation drift. The father/founder worked his butt off to build the dealership. His son enjoys the life of a millionaire and gives some effort. His son, however, blows off the whole thing and squanders three generations of wealth. My friend has seen this enough to note it and consider it a pattern. You can leave your son the gold of a work ethic.

One generation can exchange the gold of faithful fatherhood for the bronze of irresponsible parenting. God has no grandchildren, just children. Each generation must reach the next generation. I have held the hand of men who were dying, some of them rich. Not one of them ever said, "Swan, I wish I had just kept one more late appointment at the office." The biggest fatherhood regret is the neglect of their family. They want the years back. Blessed is that father who can, on his deathbed, thank God that he cared for his family and was a more spiritual man than secular man. Your clients will not be present when you take your last breath. Your family will. Do not exchange gold for bronze.

In the ancient world the people called alchemists tried to turn all sorts of stuff into gold. They had secret formulas for turning base metals into gold. It was a hoax, but they tried. The grace of God can enable you this Father's Day to start where you are in life. God is always willing to start in the precious moment called NOW. Nothing can keep you from showing your faith to your family NOW, even if you are just beginning. Nothing can keep you from showing love to your children NOW, even if you have been a father of neglect. The good news of the gospel is the promise that you can start NOW.

PAUSE TO PONDER
I Peter 1 :3-9

"Blessed be the God and Father of our Lord Jesus Christ, who according to His great mercy has caused us to be born again to a living hope through the resurrection of Jesus Christ from the dead, ⁴ to obtain an inheritance which is imperishable, undefiled, and will not fade away, reserved in heaven for you, ⁵ who are protected by the power of God through faith for a salvation ready to be revealed in the last time. ⁶ In this you greatly rejoice, even though now for a little while, if necessary, you have been distressed by various trials, ⁷ so that the proof of your faith, being more precious than gold which perishes though tested by fire, may be found to result in praise, glory, and honor at the revelation of Jesus Christ; ⁸ and though you have not seen Him, you love Him, and though you do not see Him now, but believe in Him, you greatly rejoice with joy inexpressible and full of glory, ⁹ obtaining as the outcome of your faith, the salvation of your souls."

MONDAY

Share something by example about your faith with your children. Send an email, order a book and send it to a son, or call one of them.

TUESDAY

Face squarely the faith of your parents, if you saw that, and consider how you are passing that on.

WEDNESDAY

Do something to spend time with your kids today. Make one less call, come home early, or give them the evening for something silly.

THURSDAY

Remember that God is your heavenly Father. He chose that for a reason. Ask Him to show you how to be a Father.

FRIDAY

Get outside yourself and encourage another guy, one who thinks he has blown it, how to begin to be a good father.

CHAPTER 25

OUR FATHER

In the great lottery of fathers, I was certainly a winner. We do not get to select our fathers. He is one of the two people (Mom and Dad) who most shape our lives, and is a given. Just as we do not get to select our height, color of our eyes or our native athletic ability, we do not get to select our fathers. I recognize that the very word "father" gives pain to so many people. To some it does not evoke anything positive at all. Martin Luther could hardly pray "Our Father" because of the awful relationship he had with his own father, who despised him for becoming a priest rather than a lawyer.

Jesus gave you the way to talk with God in His Model Prayer (Matthew 6:9-13). Everything hinges on the reality of the very first word in that prayer, "Father." By that word, Jesus means that God is more like a very good father than He is like anything else. Jesus did not begin His prayer by saying, "Our CEO, our Commander, our Creator" or any other words that might have been used. In the Old Testament God is called a Rock, a Shield, and a Fortress. But

Jesus did not begin His prayer with any of those words. He began the prayer with the words, "Our Father."

If that is not true, nothing else in the prayer matters. If our world and the universe does not really have the Father that Jesus embodied, we are already up a creek. Just today I read that human consciousness is simply the result of the vibrations of atoms. The materialistic, rationalistic, and anti-supernatural who rule most academies and influence our culture do not believe there is a heavenly Father. For them, the heavens are empty, and no one is there. Sigmund Freud famously stated that we invented God as a father because of the random cruelty of a harsh world.

We need to admit that when you look at the world with a level gaze, it looks random. A baby is born without limbs, a tsunami hits a beach, a ferry hits a rock, an elderly lady dies with painful cancer, a truck runs over a child in the street…and on and on and on. The brutal fact is this: If you look at the world without looking at Jesus, the world does not look like it has a father. It looks like a total mess.

The only grounds anyone has to believe there is a heavenly Father is the person of the Lord Jesus Christ. It is only your faith in His word about the Father that enables you ever to believe there really is a Father who cares, who feels, who loves, and who knows. *The only reason we can believe there is a heavenly Father is because Jesus Christ told us to pray this way.* There is no other reason to believe there is someone like a wonderful Father in heaven apart from the Lord Jesus Christ.

Every grown man worth the name has to make his mind up about this or he is dishonest with himself. If you believe life is nothing but a dog-eat-dog context for a few miserable years and then they put you in a box and bury you, that will impact everything in your miserable life. You will be suspicious, guilty, mad, and distant from what life is about. If you believe the Father that Jesus told about really reigns, you will trust, lose your guilt, get over being mad and have real relationships. All of that depends on whether or not you believe what Jesus said and embodied about God. It is a Jesus question. You believe what He said, or you face a cold grave and an empty void. Every man worthy of the name needs to face that and answer the question, "Is Jesus the true representative of a Father?"

What about the awful stuff in life? *Everything that comes from His hands must go through His hands.* You leave the doctor with prostate cancer, you lose your job, your child goes to jail, or your wife runs off with her golf teacher. All of that must pass through His hands even though it did not come from His hands. Nothing that happens to you does not have a purpose from the hands of the Father. That purpose may refine you, cause you to throw your independent worldly life into the Father's hands or even make you cry out to the Father for the first time in your life and really mean it. According to Henry Kissinger, Richard M. Nixon wound up in a fetal position on the floor of the Oval Office the last days of Watergate asking Kissinger, a secular Jew, to pray with him. If you value the immortal soul of a man, it was worth it for Nixon's immortal soul if all of it caused him to turn to the Father. How God weighs life and how you weigh it are not only not the same, they are different, not in degree but in kind. God intends to *use* what He does not *cause* to make you fit for eternity with Him. That is why you can call Him Father.

PAUSE TO PONDER
Matthew 6 :9-13

"Pray, then, in this way:

'Our Father, who is in heaven,

Hallowed be Your name.

[10] Your kingdom come.

Your will be done,

On earth as it is in heaven.

[11] Give us this day our daily bread.

[12] And forgive us our debts, as we also have

forgiven our debtors.

[13] And do not lead us into temptation,

but deliver us from evil."

MONDAY

Start this day with the word *FATHER*. View everything that
comes your way today from the hands of the Father that
Jesus described. Write it on a Post-it Note if you have to, but
remember it.

TUESDAY

When you read the headlines or watch them on cable news,
ask what a Father might do to use what you are hearing about.

WEDNESDAY

Submit the largest problem you have today to the Father.
Imagine Him with an inbox that says *FATHER*. Put it in His box.

THURSDAY

In an imaginative prayer, picture God coming to you in the
times of your life's deepest hurts from the past. Imagine a
loving, warm, embracing Father walking into the scene and
walking through it and out of it beside you.

FRIDAY

You are surrounded with people who need the Father. Steve
Green sang the haunting song, *People Need the Lord*. At the
end of broken dreams, they do. Google the words to this song
and listen to or read them as a devotional today.

CALIBER IN CHRIST – CHRIST IN THE CALIBER

By using his imagination as a young shipman, Sam Colt carved his very first wooden model of a revolving cylinder handgun. He later perfected a working version of the revolver pistol with the repetitive firing capabilities that would be patented in England and France in 1935 and shortly thereafter in the U.S.

Little did he know on those rough seas that his creation would be the most effective and complimentary tool that America would use in shaping its manifest destiny into what we have today. As well, it became the one tool of defense that would give us MEN excitement, pride and a sense of patriotic security.

Have you ever watched a so-called "western movie" that left you empty, sad and angry? That's because that Western movie was a full-scale drama or 1800 romantic piece of cinema that did NOT have guns, gunfire, horse-chase scenes or the good guy providing a 6-foot grave for the enemy by using the big iron on his hip.

Sadly, this tragedy towards men has happened in America. We know because we all have been blessed by gun-carrying heroes such as John Wayne, Wyatt Earp (Kurt Russell), Matthew Quigley (Tom Selleck), Clint Eastwood, Jimmy Stewart, Roy Rogers, The Lone Ranger and Robert Duvall in all his war/western classics. You and I both remember where we were when we first saw John Wayne take up for his boys in *The Cowboys* and fought Bruce Dern. We both can pinpoint that feeling we got when we heard Doc Holiday say "I'm your Huckleberry" or of course, when Eastwood asked the most famous question in man movie history while firmly controlling that 44 magnum: "You've got to ask yourself a question: 'Do I feel lucky?' Well do ya, punk?"

Men since the beginning of time have always been prone to express their manhood and "power of self" through an object of destruction. For cavemen, it was the humble stick, branch or rock. Sticks turned into spears, spears into swords, branches into arrows and rocks turned into objects to launch through slingshots, catapults, etc. The weapon evolution continued with the concept of tubes and barrels filled with combustible powder and a projectile. This concept was a reality with the creation-knowledge of wood stock pieces, barrels, stocks, igniters, burning ember pieces, capsules and the responsibility of the multiple "locks" (later would be hammers) that had to be forced forward to ignite the contraption for successful firing.

As it is, sadly we do not have enough time to go through the history of weaponry, but you get the gist of the flow of how we got to the modern weapons of today. Men continued to seek out the fastest, most powerful, aggressive and systematic way to be able to destroy, defend and deter enemies from causing harm. Isaiah 2:4 speaks to this.

Let your mind leave that in the past and travel to today. Today men care mostly about the CALIBER of the weapon. At least I do. The Calibers most commonly used are .380 ACP, 9mm, .45, 10mm, .357 Magnum, .38 Special and .22.

These calibers are different in size and travel. They can only be fired through a certain barrel that accommodates its size and density. Some are intended for close range, some for long range. Some are very destructive while others are enough to just royally tick off a perpetrator. The differences in each caliber also provides the distinction between the recoil.

But let's take a look at something that would probably put us men in our place when it comes to our sense of faith, manhood, security, protection and overall sense of self. Our Caliber in Christ! When it comes to true faith, security and manhood, do we find that in our inner mental state of mind? By the caliber of our pistol, the amount of ammo, magazines and knowledge we have to impress our 2nd Amendment-loving gun range buddies? While I am a true believer and active in arming myself as a responsible law-abiding citizen, my true security, faith and self-worth must be in The Caliber of Christ *first* before anything else. No matter how attractive and sexy looking that gun caliber may be behind a gun shop window, my trust must be in Christ alone.

Let's talk about David, who had his faith, security and self-worth in God Almighty. In return, God provided David with the ability to use his weapon of choice in the form of a slingshot with a caliber of a stone. No clue of the size of that stone but won't that be something cool to see when we get to heaven and browse the Biblical Weapons Museum?

What about Moses? God provided him the weapon of the staff to part the sea. Sampson's weapon of choice was the jawbone of a donkey, which heavily decreased the Philistine army. God provided Sampson that simple weapon to accomplish that feat. Joshua used the most modern weaponry and armor to defeat and do God's will.

Point being, weapons can be as small as a stone, as unique as a donkey's southern facial hardware, a stick in the woods, or a heavy 50 Cal machine gun. It doesn't matter to Christ what caliber of bullet you have, what matters to Christ is the amount faith, love and trust you put in Him and the amount of time you spend with Him on a daily basis. The important thing is how much daily training we men exercise to be fully equipped with the weapons we need in our spirit (Psalm 144:1-2).

Weapons need attention. It is important for us to take apart, clean, lubricate, wipe down and fire your weapon of choice often on a routine basis for it to be effective. It is the same way with our faith as Christians. We give our spiritual weapons attention in daily Bible reading, prayer, socializing with fellow believers and communicating our faith in a non-aggressive way towards the unbeliever.

Doing this on a routine basis will enhance our "precision" in peace, it will heighten our "awareness" in attitude and it will prepare us men to be fully equipped with the Armor that God offers to us in Ephesians 6. Jesus Christ is the most powerful, sustaining and reliable source we have all the time. He is with YOU. He is with ME. He wants you to be fully armed and protected with His love, forgiveness, grace and mercy. He can and will get you through any situation. He will give you the "firepower" you need to endure a divorce, a relapse, a job loss, a diagnosis, a moral failure or any outward or inner failure that you will experience, if you haven't already. HE is constantly equipping your heart. He does not need to be reloaded or upgraded. He is the best weapon us MEN will ever have in our lives. Get yourself armed & ready for the daily fight against our ever-constant enemy. Our Caliber in Christ will grow in accuracy as we fully rely on Him.

PAUSE TO PONDER
II CORINTHIANS 10 :4-5

"…⁴ for the weapons of our warfare are not of the flesh, but divinely powerful for the destruction of fortresses.⁵ We are destroying arguments and all arrogance raised against the knowledge of God, and we are taking every thought captive to the obedience of Christ."

MONDAY (CARRYING)

Read Ephesians 6:10-18. Write out each armored piece. Beside each one, write out your thoughts on how Jesus will protect you through that piece of armor and how that piece of armor will help you today in whatever things you are experiencing.

TUESDAY (RANGE)

Read Psalm 144:1-2. Know your target and be efficient in your accuracy. Spend a good 30 minutes in prayer, reading out loud this verse. Memorize it and let it be a part of your prayer time either in closing or beginning. It's a great verse of realization of how powerful God is. Memorization only increases our "range" and "accuracy" in Biblical strength.

WEDNESDAY (STOCK UP)

What particular areas in your life do you need more of today? Do you need to laugh, rest, work around the house or take some time to reconnect with some old buddies who may need some encouragement? Stocking up on soul needs is necessary.

THURSDAY (KNOWLEDGE)

What if a man came up to you NOW and asked you "Who is Jesus? Why do you believe in Him? What does it take to be saved?"

Do you know how you would answer? Do you have enough Biblical reference and accurate information as to who Jesus is and why you choose to be called a Christian and follow Him to give a straight answer? Knowledge is key. It is not very hard to know if a gun owner really knows about guns or not, just by a few simple questions and observing his safety measure and how he handles his weapon correctly and safely.

Are you just comfortable enough with your own knowledge and the sermons you hear? Read the Word, get involved in a men's group, listen to Christian podcasts weekly and start loading your mind with the knowledge you need.

FRIDAY (CLEANING)

JAMES 1:21 says, *"Therefore put away all filthiness and rampant wickedness and receive with meekness the implanted word, which is able to save your souls."*

Use today as the day that you have an intense inner cleaning. Read James and pray that God reveals to you the areas that you need the most cleaning and maintenance on within your personal, professional and social life.

What people, distractions, social media, TV or bad routines do you need to put away in order to be cleaned and fresh for the weekend ahead?

What actions can you perform that will 100% put these negative things away in order for you to be the man that Jesus wants you to be today?

YOU NEED AN EMPTY FRAME

Bobbie Bowden coached Florida State 1976-2009, a remarkable tenure in a profession known for shorter employment. When he came to the school, the great Christian coach inherited a football program on the verge of extinction. He left a successful program he built at West Virginia for a patent unlikelihood. Yet he succeeded beyond his own imagination.

After winning seasons, bowl games, and accolades, he lacked one achievement: a national championship. To remind himself of that, he kept an empty picture frame on his desk. The frame sat there, staring back at him and reminding him that he had yet to put a picture in the frame. Finally, in 1993, both the Associated Press and the Coaches Poll named the Seminoles the national champs. Coach Bowden finally put a picture into the empty frame that sat on his desk.

Do you have an empty frame? Is your life moving towards something in the future of worth and value that you would like to frame? Life is not only pushed from the past, but pulled by the future. Goals before you pull you towards them as well aspirations from the past push you in the same direction. You need an empty frame, a goal yet to be reached.

Paul, the follower of Jesus, spoke of just that when he exclaimed, "I press toward the mark for the upward calling of God in Christ Jesus" (Philippians 3:14). He had founded churches all over the Empire. He had written most of his 13 letters in the New Testament. He had witnessed the conversion of thousands. He found a place as a peer among the eyewitnesses of Jesus' earthly life. Yet he was not satisfied. He pressed on. He had an empty frame. There was another Timothy out there somewhere. Around some corner there was another Apollos to be discovered and encouraged. Yet another Lydia on a business trip was waiting by another river somewhere. He still wanted to put a picture in the empty frame.

The empty frame enables you to live with discipline. You do not fill empty frames resting on your laurels. Bowden did not thrive at Florida State all those years by living an undisciplined life. He risked, he strived, and he imagined. The empty frame enables you to persevere. An old word has been revived in a new age: grit. That is the quality that enables you to go on, persist, get up again when you are knocked down, and press on.

Bowden did not stop striving when he finally put a picture of a National Championship in the frame. He went on to do it again. Today, at 89 years of age, he can look back not at one but two pictures in such frames. He achieved and then achieved again. And he did all of that while retaining a strong, outspoken Christian witness.

Is there an empty frame in your life? Does a victory yet to be won sit on your desk framed by expectation but awaiting fulfillment? At some stage most men stop aspiring. They retire, sit back, vegetate, and do not last long. Achievement is in the past and aspiration has no place other than getting up in the morning. There is no empty frame awaiting them. Life has different empty frames. Someone has said that in your 20's, you dream of making love, in your 30's you dream of getting a promotion, in your 40's, you dream of making money, in your 50's, you dream of making the corner office, and then in your 60's, you just dream of making it to the end. Life stalls out. Dreams disappear. A dull satisfaction takes over.

You always need an empty frame for life to have meaning. What goes in that frame may change. At 60, it may be investing your life in a second career of service. At 70, it may be a final mentoring of a young man. At 80, it may be refining your character into an ultimate Christlikeness. You sand down the rough edges, polish the virtues, live constantly in prayer until you open your eyes on the other side. Whatever it may be, keep an empty frame in your life and God will bless it with something fulfilling. You will likely live longer and better.

PAUSE TO PONDER
Joshua 1 :1-9

"Now it came about after the death of Moses the servant of the Lord, that the Lord spoke to Joshua the son of Nun, Moses' servant, saying, 2 "Moses My servant is dead; so now arise, cross this Jordan, you and all this people, to the land which I am giving to them, to the sons of Israel. 3 Every place on which the sole of your foot steps, I have given it to you, just as I spoke to Moses. 4 From the wilderness and this Lebanon, even as far as the great river, the river Euphrates, all the land of the Hittites, and as far as the Great Sea toward the setting of the sun will be your territory. 5 No one will be able to oppose you all the days of your life. Just as I have been with Moses, I will be with you; I will not desert you nor abandon you. 6 Be strong and courageous, for you shall give this people possession of the land which I swore to their fathers to give them. 7 Only be strong and very courageous; be careful to do according to all the Law which Moses My servant commanded you; do not turn from it to the right or to the left, so that you may achieve success wherever you go. 8 This Book of the Law shall not depart from your mouth, but you shall meditate on it day and night, so that you may be careful to do according to all that is written in it; for then you will make your way prosperous, and then you will achieve success. 9 Have I not commanded you? Be strong and courageous! Do not be terrified nor dismayed, for the Lord your God is with you wherever you go."

MONDAY

Think of persons you know in your own circle and network who have an empty frame they still strive for. At the same time, remember those who just gave up on life and sat. Which do you want?

TUESDAY

Think of others like Bowden who never gave up on the empty frame, who persevered until the picture finally emerged.

WEDNESDAY

Consider some biblical characters who lived to fill an empty frame. Who would they be besides Paul? Moses lived to be 120 and his life contributed to the end.

THURSDAY

Ask God to give you a vision for your empty frame. What does He wish you to strive for in your own future?

FRIDAY

Share this vision with a trusted friend and prayer partner. Ask them to join in keeping you accountable.

EAT THE BOOK

Something about us likes to watch, or at least get a report, from eating contests. On Coney Island each July 4 is a hotdog eating competition. The record is 69 hotdogs in 10 minutes. If you go to the other coast, in San Jose at the taco eating contest, the record is 101 tacos in eight minutes. Not be outdone, in Clearwater, Florida, you may try to break the wing-eating record. So far it stands at 184 wings in ten minutes. As you might expect, the oyster eating contest is in New Orleans. Would you like to challenge the record of 46 dozen – that is 46x12 = 552 – in 10 minutes?

Then there are the pitiable victims of an eating disorder called Pica. Twin sisters in Bradford, UK, suffer from this challenge. Adele likes to eat candles when she is anxious and her sister, Anita, goes in for used books. She does not care about the dust and markings on the old tomes. Just give her a used Agatha Christi and she is in culinary heaven. These are not children; the twins were 50 when the report came out in a British paper.

Would it surprise you that God once ordered a prophet to eat a book? Consider these words from the mystical prophet Ezekiel:

He said to me, O mortal, eat what is offered to you; eat this scroll, so I opened my mouth, and he gave me the scroll to eat. He said to me, Mortal, eat this scroll that I give you and fill your stomach with it. Then I ate it; and in my mouth it was as sweet as honey (**EZEKIEL 3:1-3**).

Old Zeke was a prophet to the Jewish refugees who were exported to Iraq for seventy years. After he ate the book, he had to sit still for seven days to digest it (Ezekiel 3:15). Then he told the Jews what they needed to hear. You can read what was in the book in Ezekiel. Often in the Christian church and experience, the idea of eating the word of God is used as a figure of speech. "Break thou the bread of life, dear Lord to me."

In 1877 at the Chautauqua in western New York, Mary Latherbury wrote these beautiful words:

Break now the bread of life, dear Lord, to me,
As once you broke the loaves beside the sea.
Beyond the sacred page I seek you, Lord;
My spirit waits for you, O living Word.

Bless your own word of truth, dear Lord, to me,
As when you blessed the bread by Galilee.
Then shall all bondage cease, all fetters fall;
And I shall find my peace, my All in all!

The thought in Ezekiel, and in this immortal hymn, suggests

personal reflection on the Word of God. Sometimes this is called ruminating on the Word. A ruminating animal, such as a cow, chews on its cud, swallows it, and then brings it back up again. Although that might not be appetizing to consider, it is a strong figure of speech when applied to the Word of God. We men spend some time reading stuff that is necessary or fun to read. We must read some stuff for work. We enjoy reading sports reports on Facebook, or if you an old codger like me, in the daily newspaper. I turn to the sports first. That makes me happier than the front page. Yet the same God of Ezekiel also tells you "eat the book."

I know. If you start reading the Bible in Leviticus, it only gets tougher in Numbers. Get yourself a plan to read Scripture that is comfortable for you. A simple search will yield a dozen different plans to read the Bible. Just get a plan, some plan. Halitosis is better than no breath at all. Then, make a deal with God that you will not spend a day without reading His Word.

The devil will do everything he can invent to keep you from the Word of God. Just try to read it daily and you will find out. When you sit down to read the Word, the devil will tell you to clean out the garage, start a new filing system, or get the weeds out of the back yard – anything but read the Word of God. Read it when you feel like it. More importantly, read it when you do NOT feel like it. On the morning when three cups of coffee did not wake you up, you have a headache, a report due, and are generally mad at the world, you will be astonished at how He can meet you in the word. Eat the book.

Also, if you miss a day, don't decide you are a spiritual failure, beyond help, and going to hell in a gasoline suit. Just get back on the diet the next day. Eat the book.

PAUSE TO PONDER
I Peter 1 :24-25

"For, all flesh is like grass,

And all its glory is like the flower of grass.

The grass withers,

And the flower falls off,

25 But the word of the Lord endures forever."

And this is the word which was preached to you."

MONDAY

Get on the web and enter "Bible reading plans". Pick one and get started NOW. Don't wait for the perfect plan or to feel spiritual. Get with it, today.

TUESDAY

Chew on one or two verses from the passage you read. This is not a hotdog eating contest. You are not trying to beat the next guy by speed-reading Habakkuk. God will put some words in personal italics for you. Camp out there.

WEDNESDAY

Pray over some words you just read. Ask God to make them sweet in your mouth.

THURSDAY

After your time in the Word, commit to God to go out and live it today. Do something that God tells you to do from the Word you read.

FRIDAY

Without being holier than thou, find someone else to share a sentence from the Word. You do not have to sound like a preacher with a boom box. Just casually slip a phrase from the Word in your conversation.

IT TAKES SCISSORS TO
GET INTO SCISSORS

Sometimes I go to the fabric store with my wife. There isn't much there that interests me, but I go along to be a good sport. The other day I made my annual trip to that store. While she looked at yarn, and fabric, and beads, and other strange stuff, my eyes fell on a package of scissors. There were three different sized scissors sealed into the package. I could buy three green, orange, or blue scissors. Being a Baylor Bear, I bought the green scissors.

Here is where the story gets weird. I need to make a confession. I am not good at opening stuff. Cans, medicine, peanuts, and scissors sealed into packages with heavy gauge molded plastic all defy my efforts. In the case of the scissors sealed into plastic that might as well have been welded shut like a steel gate, I needed scissors in order to get into the scissors. I know that sounds pathetic, but that was my problem. In order to get into scissors, I needed scissors.

When I finally found a rusty pair of scissors in the back of the most unlikely drawer in the house, I used them to get into the new scissors. Without those old scissors, I did not even know how to get started. My challenge was that basic. I could not cut through the heavy gauged plastic molding to get the new scissors without finding an old pair of scissors.

After that strange episode, I reflected on just how strange it was. I already had part of the solution somewhere. It was like what I was trying to find. I just had to find how to start. Isn't that the fact about most things men face? I know I need to get it done. Somewhere there is something that could help me get it done. I just must find the way to get started.

For most things we face in life, it is getting started that is the hard thing and the main thing. The yard is overgrown with weeds; I need to pull the first one. The garage needs painting; I need to open a can of paint. I must write a report on the last business trip; I need to write the first word. I need to spend more time with my son; I just need to clear my calendar. Anything good in life depends on the energy, focus, and drive to do the first thing about it. We fail at so many things because we refuse to find a way to take the first step. Dissertations are not written, sheds are not built, and gardens are not planted because we cannot write the first word, hammer the first nail, or till up the first row of soil. We need some Nike theology: Just Do It.

Paul indicates the goodness of God in this regard. He recounts that God works in us to will and do His good pleasure. Whatever we face, big or little, monumental or mundane, God is with us to help us take the first step. You are not on your own to get started. God is the Lord of initiative. Jesus Himself said, "Whatever I see the Father doing, I am doing."

The first thing we need to do to have the energy, drive, determination, and thrust we need, is to rest with the Father, who is already working. There is a good reason the Bible begins with the resounding words: "In the beginning..." God is always there in the beginning of anything worthwhile.

God was there when the first stone of an enormous cathedral was laid. He is there when you are about to pick up the phone to make your first sales call. He is there when you drive the first nail, argue the first sentence of a lawsuit, or enter the first numbers into a complicated chart of accounts. The life of faith reckons that He is always there before you start, even when you are looking for scissors to open scissors.

PAUSE TO PONDER
JOHN 5 :19-24

"Therefore Jesus answered and was saying to them, "Truly, truly, I say to you, the Son can do nothing of Himself, unless it is something He sees the Father doing; for whatever the Father does, these things the Son also does in the same way. 20 For the Father loves the Son and shows Him all things that He Himself is doing; and the Father will show Him greater works than these, so that you will be amazed. 21 For just as the Father raises the dead and gives them life, so the Son also gives life to whom He wishes. 22 For not even the Father judges anyone, but He has given all judgment to the Son, 23 so that all will honor the Son just as they honor the Father. The one who does not honor the Son does not honor the Father who sent Him.24 "Truly, truly, I say to you, the one who hears My word, and believes Him who sent Me, has eternal life, and does not come into judgment, but has passed out of death into life."

MONDAY

Look at your calendar. What is the first thing that needs to
get done that you cannot start? Give that to the Lord who is
already there and working. Do it.

TUESDAY

Inventory your list of tasks and find one that you started and
stopped, began and discarded, and yet you must do it.
Ask God to help you pick up again, right now.

WEDNESDAY

Whatever it is that you must do today, God has already made
provision for you to do everything that belongs to His will in
your life. Look for what He has already given.

THURSDAY

It's hard by the yard but a cinch by the inch.
Start with something small today and take a little beginning
step with the help of God. Maybe you need to stop a habit.
Kick it for one hour. Do not worry about the rest of your life.
Start with the first hour.

FRIDAY

Find a buddy who cannot even think of starting something he
must get done. Sit with him. Help him take the first step.

CARS: YOUNG AND OLD GUYS

Sometimes websites ask for a personal memory to provide an additional level of security. One of those questions involves your first car. I have no problem remembering that my first car was a 1955 Ford Fairlane. I bought it for the enormous sum of $150. Since the paint looked like the side of a forgotten barn in a Kansas wheat field, I paid the immortal Earl Shieb $29.95 to paint it. His job looked like a Michelangelo oil painting to my high school eyes. It was a standard shift and worked best going downhill. Parallel parking required an astronaut's skills.

At the same time, I also began to dream of another car. The older I got, the vision got as sharp as a Gillette five-blade razor: I wanted a muscle car that captured the attractive females like tuna fish attracts a cat and honey magnetizes flies. I wanted the roar of its 400 HP engine to enthrall my buddies. That car was as clear a vision to me as the Revelation was to the Apostle John. I could see it in the sky all day and in my dreams at night.

Now that I am a mature gentleman and have bought, driven, repaired, insured, and wrecked many kinds of cars, I am reverting. My 1955 Ford Fairlane is now a classic. I would love to have it back, repaint it again, and go to the junkyard to find authentic parts. To drive to the airport in my restored 1955 would be a bigger thrill than to buy another predictable SUV that is as common as athlete's foot in a locker room.

Cars remind me of other things from my past that would be fun to bring back. I wish I could run out of the door with my grandkids to the ice cream truck playing its Jack-in-the-Box tune. I would like to sit with them in front of an old TV and let the original Pacman eat little dots. Just one Saturday morning, I would like to sit with my grandson and watch Captain Kangaroo or Fury, the story of a horse and the boy who loved him, followed by Sky King and Penny. Old seems better than new right now. Just ask Coca-Cola how their New Coke worked out! They call the good old one "Classic" now.

In a similar way, living the Christian life is like all of that. The first things you learn are the most important things. The old Apostle John, who lived to be somewhere around 100, wrote the Christians at Ephesus, "Let that remain in you that you heard from the beginning" (1 John 2:24).

The first things you learned about the Christian faith will always be the most important. When you are about to go into the life beyond, you will not be thinking about marginal, secondary stuff. You will be thinking about the first things. God is. He exists. Jesus is His Son. He shed His blood for your sins. You trusted Him. He will take you across to the other side. You will be with Him forever and ever. Those first things you learned about God and Jesus will be the most important things to you at the end.

It's like painting. All colors originate from the three primary colors: red, green, and blue. All other colors come from combinations of those primary colors. Humans can mix the primary colors to make other colors, but humans did not invent the primary colors. They are givens in the green of the forest, the blue of the sky or the red of your blood.

Knowing more and more stuff about God is like that. The primary things are God, His Son Jesus, and your faith. You can mix and re-mix, but you never learn anything more important than those first things. I can guarantee you, when you are about to move upstairs forever, you will not be thinking about exotic theological tidbits. You will be thinking about the primary things.

When the most famous theologian of the 20th century, Karl Barth, visited the USA from Switzerland, a reporter asked him to state his most profound thought. He shocked the sophisticated crowd around him at a Chicago meeting by saying, "Jesus loves me, this I know, because the Bible tells me so."

When Paul wrote the Colossians, a church in today's Turkey, he warned them that they were getting too fancy in their theology. They were adding all kinds of other things to the simple basic story of the Lord Jesus Christ. Paul reminded the Colossians of the supremacy and sufficiency of Christ and Christ alone. He created all things and He is the Head of His Church.

That is the reason that the whole world sings Hillsong's "Christ Alone, Cornerstone." That's the reason we sang in earlier years, "My hope is built on nothing less, that Jesus' blood and righteousness." An elite theologian said, "The existential angst of spiritually dialectic humans requires the propitiatory atonement of the Chalcedonian Christ." An old farmer in his Dickies Overalls responded, "I need to be covered by the blood of Jesus." Keep it simple.

The Bible reverts just like that. The first book, Genesis, begins with humans in a garden with a tree. They failed in that garden at that tree. The end of the last book, Revelation, ends in a new garden with new trees, for the healing of the nations. The reason you can get from the old tree to the new trees is because of that tree in the middle, the Cross. Just like wanting old cars back, we need to go back to the basics we learned first.

PAUSE TO PONDER
JOHN 3 :16-21

"For God so loved the world, that He gave His only Son, so that everyone who believes in Him will not perish but have eternal life. 17 For God did not send the Son into the world to judge the world, but so that the world might be saved through Him. 18 The one who believes in Him is not judged; the one who does not believe has been judged already, because he has not believed in the name of the only Son of God. 19 And this is the judgment, that the Light has come into the world, and people loved the darkness rather than the Light; for their deeds were evil. 20 For everyone who does evil hates the Light, and does not come to the Light, so that his deeds will not be exposed. 21 But the one who practices the truth comes to the Light, so that his deeds will be revealed as having been performed in God."

MONDAY

Remember the preachers and Sunday School teachers who taught you the first, basic things you ever knew about God, Jesus and the Christian life. Thank God for them. Call their names and praise His name.

TUESDAY

Where have you made complicated what God has made simple? The basics of faith, hope, and love will never be replaced. Ask God to give you the faith to love, the hope to believe, and the belief to hope.

WEDNESDAY

Think of some of some old stuff around your house, in your garage, or in your attic that reminds you of the basic stuff you learned when you were a kid. A brittle baseball glove, your dad's old tool box, or an old fishing reel would be examples. When you think of those old things, what do they remind you of about your heritage and legacy?

THURSDAY

Get somewhere quiet and alone. Spend five minutes each on the primary words of faith: faith, hope, and love. What did you learn about them at the beginning? What do they mean now?

FRIDAY

In a bull session with some friends, remember precious things from way back, things that shaped your life and built your soul.

CHAPTER 31

RUN, CATCH, BLOCK, HIT

A friend is the pastor of a famed Chicago Bear running back. He is second only to the legendary Walter Payton as a star back for the Bears. The focus, discipline, energy, and fitness of the man is astonishing. He explains that a back must be able to run with the ball, catch the ball, block, and take a hit. He must be able in four disciplines.

For a real Christian man, life presents the urgent need for the same disciplines in the spiritual realm. The Apostle Paul often compared the Christian life to running, wrestling, blocking the fiery darts of the devil, and taking hits.

The Christian life is compared to a race. In 1 Corinthians 9, Paul insisted that all Christians run. He exhorts you in Philippians 3 to press on, as if in a sprint pressing towards the tape. The longest race run as an all-out sprint is the 100 meter. The best athletes in the world are panting, hearts pounding, hands reaching, and lungs heaving at the 98th, 99th, and 100th meter. Paul never compared the Christian life to sitting in your lazy chair. It has about it all the discipline needed for an agonizing race. In the famous Olympic and Artemesian games of the ancient world, the athletes would train strictly for ten months. In the Olympics today, athletes will go to Colorado Springs in order to take .01 seconds off their time. It is serious, strenuous pursuit. So also is the Christian life. It is not for slackers.

The Christian life may be compared to catching a football. The timing, pace, route, and vision involved in an NFL catch make the best athletes strain for all they can accomplish. So much of the Christian life relates to the right use of time and using the right time. The Christian learns to pace life, waiting on God. The route itself is a narrow way; Jesus said few find it. The vision required is nothing less than that provided by a new birth that enables you to see the Kingdom of God.

The Christian life must block some things. The Enemy hurls temptations, depression, distractions, weariness, and foolishness at us constantly. The victorious Christian must block these in order to persevere. When we least expect it, we must block something that could destroy life, family, career, and influence. The oncoming enemy never ceases. Blocking is part of the victorious life.

At the same time, we must be ready to take a hit. Jesus never promised a smooth ride. Every stage and level of life has its own hits. The hits early in life may involve the grosser temptation to break the laws of God. In later life the hits come at us in the form of illness, grief, and loss. Then we face the hardest hit of all – the end of life. The hits men take are relentless. Get ready for the next one.

Yet we have a Coach better than the best coach. In a sense, He is a player/coach. He took on human flesh, ran the race all the way to the Cross, caught the fiery darts of the weary one, stayed on course, and took the ultimate hit of all, our sins. Every chapter in all 16 chapters of Mark has the same word in the chapter, "way." Jesus is always on the way in Mark. Nothing can keep Him off His way. Interruptions, oppositions, demons, storms, enemies, and even His own family could not keep Him off the way. He fought the good fight and finished His course, just as Paul did.

The All-Pro defensive end for the Cleveland Browns a lifetime ago was Bill Glass. He was also an ordained minister. He started a national prison ministry. He noted that there was nothing casual about playing for the NFL. Bill said, "If you are casual in the NFL, you will get knocked on your casual can." The same is true of the Christian life. A weak, limp, lifeless, spineless, bloodless, whining and careless approach to the Christian life will not cut it. Nothing takes more of everything a man is than the Christian life.

PAUSE TO PONDER
I Corinthians 9 :24-27

"Do you not know that those who run in a race all run,

but only one receives the prize? Run in such a way that you

may win. [25] Everyone who competes in the games exercises

self-control in all things. So they do it to obtain a perishable

wreath, but we an imperishable. [26] Therefore I run in such a

way as not to run aimlessly; I box in such a way, as to avoid

hitting air; [27] but I strictly discipline my body and make it

my slave, so that, after I have preached to others, I myself

will not be disqualified."

MONDAY

Consider your life as a race. Do you see it as a sprint? Is it a 10,000 meter? Where do you think you are on the race? Are you worried about those behind you? Are you in your lane?

TUESDAY

What has life thrown at you in the past that you did not expect? What is it throwing at you today? Are you ready?

WEDNESDAY

Victorious Christian living means blocking stuff coming at you. What do you need to block out of your life to stay on course? Can you identify something you have spent a lifetime blocking? Are there new assaults at this chapter of life?

THURSDAY

What kind of hits can you expect today? Are you ready? Can you play the game of life without a penalty?

FRIDAY

Find a friend who has changed lanes, dropped the ball, slipped off a block, and is taking hits. Speak a word of encouragement, confidence, and faith into that life.

CHAPTER 32

AN OX, A DONKEY AND "GOTCHA"

"You shall not give a false report; do not join your hand with a wicked person to be a malicious witness. You shall not follow the crowd in doing evil, nor shall you testify in a dispute so as to join together with a crowd in order to pervert justice; nor shall you show favor to a poor person in his dispute."

"If you encounter your enemy's ox or his donkey wandering away, you must return it to him. If you see the donkey of one who hates you lying helpless under its load, you shall not leave it helpless for its owner; you must arrange the load with him."
EXODUS 23: 1-5 NASB VERSION

Now, I know what you are about to think: "Swan, I haven't seen a runaway ox in weeks. It's been longer than that since I saw a donkey that couldn't complete a bench press." Sometimes stories about oxen and donkeys, however, are more than about beasts.

They may be about you and the guy in the next cubicle, or your neighbor with the barking dog. It is any situation that presents a perfect "gotcha" moment. You can get even. No one would even see it. You could pull off the grand payback. Karma could use you to catch up with the guy who deserves it. You can laugh up your sleeve. It's just your little secret. You got even.

Here's the problem: God told Moses right before He gave him the Ten Commandments that His people should not go for the gotcha moment. Jesus made it even tougher: "Love your enemies and pray for those who persecute you" (Matthew 5:43). When the barking dog of your grouchy neighbor gets hit by a speeding motorist, you take it to the vet, not kick it when it is down. When the schemer next to you at work gets what is coming, you help him with an overload of work. Hard? Yes. Necessary? If you call yourself Jesus' follower, double yes.

In the famous World War I movie, *Path to Glory*, 41-year-old Kirk Douglas plays a French military officer who is also an attorney. The movie turns around the trial of three men who were chosen at random to be killed by a firing squad as representatives of an entire battalion that refused to go over the top out of the trenches. A corrupt French general had ordered his artillery to fire on his own men to make them leave the trenches, unheard of cruelty. That same vain, pompous general ordered the three soldiers randomly chosen to be shot as examples to all the troops of the price for failure to go forward into enemy fire. In a famous movie gotcha moment, Kirk Douglas exposes the corruption of the general who ordered artillery to fire on his own men before he called for their execution. Kirk Douglas is then offered the rank of general for the gotcha. He turned it down.

By the time old Kirk, who lived to be 104, outed the corrupt general, I was saying, "Get him. Expose him. Out him." That is the normal human response when an obvious gotcha moment is at hand. Yet Kirk refused to gain by that moment. On the one hand, the general needed to be exposed. On the other hand, Kirk was unwilling to corrupt himself by accepting an award for the moment.

Life presents all of us with gotcha moments. Some people live for them, watch for them, and plot for them. You cannot be a Jesus follower and live to settle the score. There is an even bigger challenge for the Jesus follower. When you are the object of a gotcha moment, on the receiving end, you cannot retaliate. You love your enemy. That is, you willfully seek the highest good of an enemy. A friend of mine helped one colleague get a promotion over another colleague. He thought it was best for the institution. My friend wound up being evaluated by and reporting to the spurned, overlooked colleague. That rejected colleague gave the annual review to my friend and mistreated him every year for years. My humble friend never said a word and even applauded the skills of his supervisor.

The greatest gotcha moment in human history could have been when Jesus was on the Cross. One of the great Christian solos of our lives was based on Jesus' claim in Matthew 26:53, "He Could Have Called Ten Thousand Angels." He could have made a gotcha moment that Steven Spielberg could not have produced. The Son of God did not do that. He stayed on the Cross while the Pharisees, Sadducees, Herodians, Romans, Jews, and the mob all said to Him,

GOTCHA. You and I are missing hell and getting into heaven because when the mob said GOTCHA, He did not reciprocate.

Would you like a formula for personal misery? Do you want to assure that you will be an angry man until you are on your deathbed? Live your life for paybacks, gotchas, and get evens. You will have hell on earth and then more later. Let it go. Give it to Him. Believe in the justice of God. You will be happy, and God will be pleased. A famous college president told an enemy, "I've got a long memory." Then he died. I expect the last thing he wanted to hear from God was, "I've got a long memory too."

PAUSE TO PONDER
Matthew 5 :43-48

"You have heard that it was said, 'You shall love your neighbor and hate your enemy.' 44 But I say to you, love your enemies and pray for those who persecute you, 45 so that you may prove yourselves to be sons of your Father who is in heaven; for He causes His sun to rise on the evil and the good, and sends rain on the righteous and the unrighteous. 46 For if you love those who love you, what reward do you have? Even the tax collectors, do they not do the same? 47 And if you greet only your brothers and sisters, what more are you doing than others? Even the Gentiles, do they not do the same? 48 Therefore you shall be perfect, as your heavenly Father is perfect."

MONDAY

Throughout this day, watch for any potential gotcha moments at work or at home. They may involve you or you may be an observer. What happens? Is anyone happy?

TUESDAY

Inventory your own past. Identify the gotcha moments when you thought you got even. How do you feel about it now, years later? Are you pleased with yourself?

WEDNESDAY

Look for opportunities when the Enemy tells you to get even. It may be with a snarky remark, a hateful word, or a caustic look. Stop it. Don't do it. Give it to Jesus.

THURSDAY

Look for opportunities today to do good to those who do not mean good to you. Don't make it obvious. Best of all, do not even let them know who did the good. God knows.

FRIDAY

Dare to help someone who lives for revenge. Lovingly confront them. Ask them how it is working for them. Are they any happier? Speak the truth in love.

CHAPTER 33

BROKEN BONES

As an old athlete, I can tell you there are a bunch of ways to hurt your bones. Just consider a few of them:

Transverse fractures are breaks straight across the bone, usually the result of sharp, direct blows or stress fractures caused by prolonged running; they occur at a right angle to the bone's long axis. An *oblique fracture* occurs at a diagonal to the bone's long axis. A *spiral fracture* is one in which part of the bone has twisted, caused by a twisting force. Also called a *torsion fracture*. A *comminuted fracture* is when the bone has fractured into several pieces. An *avulsion fracture* is one in which a part of the bone has entirely separated from the main part of the bone. An *impacted fracture* results when bone fragments are driven into each other. A *fissure fracture* is an incomplete fracture in which the crack is only in the outer bone layer. It's also called a *hairline fracture*. A *greenstick fracture* is when only one side of a bone is broken. The bone usually has a bend to it and the fracture is located at the outside of the bend. This is common in young children.

A *comminuted fracture* is the most difficult to repair, due to the bone having fractured into numerous pieces. Multiple bone pieces require more effort to hold them together in the ideal position for healing. The body also must fill in a different matrix between the bone pieces, which are at risk of not repairing correctly due to the nature of the fracture. This type of fracture may require part of the bone to be removed and replaced by artificial/synthetic bones

The Psalmist wrote, "When I kept silent, my bones wasted away through my groaning all day long" (Psalm 32:3). Bones can be a metaphor, a figure of speech, and a way of expressing how you feel in your spirit. Some of the fractures above remind us of fractured spirits. Sometimes we have a spiritual *spiral fracture*. We do things that twist us, sometimes painfully. The old Bible word in Hebrew for *iniquity* means "twisted."

At other times we have a spiritual *avulsion fracture*. We are separated from the rest of who we are. We stand outside ourselves and say to ourselves, "How could I have done that?" We become strangers to ourselves.

At other time we have a *hairline fracture*. That is only on the surface, but it still hurts. Life does some stuff like that to us. It is not deep, but it still gives us pain.

We can also have a spiritual *comminuted fracture*. That is the worst. Multiple pieces of us have broken apart. We are like Humpty Dumpty. Financial failure can lead to domestic failure that can lead to broken homes and hearts that can lead to moral failure that also leads to social rejection and a whole lot more. Our life can be fractured into pieces. Can anyone put us back together again?

Yes. When Jesus met Legion, the crazy guy living in the cemetery, the man was fractured into pieces. A Roman legion could have 6,000 men in it. The tormented grave dweller felt as if there were 6,000 different men living inside of him. He was broken. You could see it in where he lived, how he dressed, what he said, and who he feared. He lived with dead people, was the original streaker, screamed at 100 decibels, and feared an encounter with Jesus. Yet Jesus put him back together (Mark 5).

A lifetime of ministry has led me to see that we are all fractured in many ways. Some of the hurts are hairline, but some are comminuted: deep, agonizing, terrifying, and painful. Some men try to heal the hurt with drugs and alcohol. They wake up and the pain is still there. Some men try to drown pain in sex. Wilt Chamberlain famously said that he slept with 20,000 women. Did it help? Wilt said just before he died, "Having a thousand ladies is pretty cool. I've learned in my life. I've found out that having one woman a thousand different times is more satisfying." There is a lot of pain hiding behind those final words. Other men try to hide the hurt in OCD busyness; they can never stop working, even at home when kids beg them.

There is only One and One only that can heal the comminuted fractures of life. When He was dying on the Cross, they tried to break His bones but didn't have to. He was already dead. Through His death you can be made whole. I cannot explain how that works. How can a cow eat green grass and it turns into a delicious steak on your barbecue? No one knows the answer to that. In a more profound way, no one can adequately answer how Jesus does what He does, but He does it. Millions have said so. Next one up?

PAUSE TO PONDER
GALATIANS 6 :1-3

"Brothers and sisters, even if a person is caught in any wrongdoing, you who are spiritual are to restore such a person in a spirit of gentleness; each one looking to yourself, so that you are not tempted as well. [2] Bear one another's burdens, and thereby fulfill the law of Christ. [3] For if anyone thinks that he is something when he is nothing, he deceives himself."

MONDAY

Ask yourself in honest reflection how you have been broken
in life. Face it.

TUESDAY

Ask yourself how you have broken others in life, how you have
hurt them, and fractured their spirits.

WEDNESDAY

Imagine Jesus standing in front of you with a beautiful basket.
He is inviting you to put all of the broken pieces of you as well
as others that you have broken into that basket. Literally, in
prayer, put the pieces into the His basket. Let Him have them.

THURSDAY

Again, imagine Jesus touching the broken bones of a lame man
in Scripture. See His face, imagine His hands, see the lame
man leap, and walk and rejoice. Now, imagine Jesus coming to
you, touching you and you are whole.

FRIDAY

Find someone you know who has a compound spiritual
fracture. Be His hands. Read Galatians 6:1-3 and it will tell
you how to reset a broken spirit.

CARRYING WHAT OUGHT TO BE CARRYING YOU

Sometimes the Ol' Swan's eyes play tricks. I saw a man walking down the narrow, concrete median in the middle of a six-lane city avenue. He was carrying something made of metal bars. He had on a white t-shirt and fatigue pants with a red beard. He was wobbling a little, but carrying his load. He darted off the median and lunged into the oncoming traffic. He sprinted to the curb and walked on. Out of the corner of my eye I glimpsed what he carried: a bicycle frame. It had no wheels, just the frame.

That was odd enough to provoke my attention. Rather than the bicycle carrying him he was carrying the bicycle. My racing imagination lurched into some other similar possibilities. Does a cowboy ever have to carry his horse? Does an Indian have to carry his elephant? Kids carry scooters everywhere today. There is something odd about having to carry something that ought to be carrying you.

Sometimes "religion" becomes a burden rather than a blessing. Jesus offered an alternative to that when He spoke to the burdened crowd:

Come unto me, all you that labor and are heavy laden, and I will give you rest. Take my yoke upon you and learn of me; for I am meek and lowly in heart: and you shall find rest unto your souls. For my yoke is easy and my burden is light (MATTHEW 11:29).

Jesus was not talking about rest breaks during the workday. He was addressing the predominant view of religion in His day. The Jews had subdivided the Ten Commandments into 613 negative prohibitions and positive admonitions. They insisted that to please God, you had to remember and practice all of them. For example, they argued about whether you could wear a wooden false tooth or not on the Sabbath. They debated whether slapping a fly crawling on your face was work on the Sabbath because you were hunting.

These tiny, pesky subjects became a great weight to the common folks. The Pharisees, a group of 6,000 laypersons, remembered and practiced them all. They called the other folks "people of the land." That meant folks too tired or too unable to remember 613 things each day to please God.

Jesus compared such religious hairsplitting to nonsense. In contrast, His teaching was light and life-giving. He lifted burdens. Now, His expectations were heavy in another way. He expected total commitment to Him, a first to which nothing else was a second. Yet that commitment to His words and person had a lightness about it, life and fresh wind and relief. Anyone who has turned from pleasing God by his own works to receiving the gift of eternal life knows what Jesus means.

It seems like many church folks are overly burdened with formal religious responsibilities. Will Rogers used to quip, "The state of Oklahoma builds the roads and Baptists wear them out going to meetings."

My tribe of Christians seems to look for any unfilled hour and find some religious activity to fill it. This does not seem to be the way of Jesus for the most part. He told them that His yoke fit well.

There is an old legend that the sign on Joseph's carpenter shop stated, "My yokes fit well." A carpenter made wooden yokes for oxen. If they were not sized and fitted, they would chaff and burden the ox. Joseph was known for making yokes that fit with comfort. Perhaps Jesus used the word from the carpenter shop to illustrate His own approach to discipleship. His living faith carries you; you do not have to carry a religion.

It is always a good thing to ask of religious busyness and burdens, "Is this Jesus' idea for me or am I participating in a program that is not His?" His burden is light. He came to carry you, not make you carry Him."

PAUSE TO PONDER
MATTHEW 11 :25-30

"At that time Jesus said, "I praise You, Father, Lord of heaven and earth, that You have hidden these things from the wise and intelligent, and have revealed them to infants. 26 Yes, Father, for this way was well pleasing in Your sight. 27 All things have been handed over to Me by My Father; and no one knows the Son except the Father; nor does anyone know the Father except the Son, and anyone to whom the Son determines to reveal Him."

28 "Come to Me, all who are weary and burdened, and I will give you rest. 29 Take My yoke upon you and learn from Me, for I am gentle and humble in heart, and you will find rest for your souls. 30 For My yoke is comfortable, and My burden is light."

MONDAY

Search you own heart when it comes to your life as a believer. What is a burden and what lifts burdens? Think through your calendar, commitments and causes. Which are His and which are not?

TUESDAY

Ask yourself this question: "Am I a human being or a human doing?" Jesus always puts the emphasis first on being and wholeness before you do anything.

WEDNESDAY

Without judgmentalism, consider those you know whose religious life is a burden. They are sour rather than sweet, burdened rather than blessed. Do you see yourself in this?

THURSDAY

Set a time to BE with Jesus today. You do not have to do anything. No calls to make, no cause to support, no visit to attend...just BE with Jesus in thought and rest.

FRIDAY

Gently help a burdened friend to let something specific go. Some are carrying burdens they do not have to carry. Lighten their load by telling them to let go.

A CALL TO RESCUE THE STRANDED: DUNKIRK AND YOU

In a disaster that could have ended Western Civilization, 338,226 Allied troops were stranded and cut off near a French beach May 26–June 4, 1940. The Archbishop of Canterbury called for prayer to save the army and England from Hitler's Nazi troops who could have slaughtered the trapped Allied army on the beaches. By a miracle of God, the German troops pulled back just enough to permit 861 vessels to rescue the trapped men and save the British army. Newly elected Prime Minister Winston Churchill led the gallant rescue that used many small fishing and leisure boats to cross the 21 miles from Dover to the trapped army. The "Miracle of Dunkirk" was a combination of an act of God and the cooperation of thousands of unknown men in little boats. Hitler mysteriously backed away from the Allied soldiers who were sitting ducks. A flotilla of little boats did the rest.

A 2017 movie recalled the event and introduced a new generation to the astonishing risk and divine intervention. It underscores some lessons that all men always could learn from this critical moment in recent history.

• **God can and does work behind the scenes.** There was no rational explanation of why Hitler's army would not swoop down on the helpless Allied troops at Dunkirk. It would have been total disaster for the Allied cause. Instead, Hitler's army backed away. In the same way many believe God alone saved the rest of the U.S. Pacific Fleet at the Battle of Midway due to the prayers of sailors, many believe Dunkirk was an act of divine intervention.

• **God did and does work in world history and in your history.** How many times in your own life have threats not come to pass, enemies strangely disappear, and dangers evaporate when only God could have orchestrated the circumstances? In eternity we shall encounter phenomenal stories of divine intervention that we do not see now. Angels around us, God above us, and the Spirit within us worked in ways we did not know to prearrange circumstances we did not even recognize.

• **Men can do together what looks impossible at first glance.** When Churchill called on every citizen with a boat to cross the Channel and rescue the troops, on the surface it looked like a fool's errand. The "Little Ships" began arriving on the beaches of Dunkirk on May 28, 1940. One little craft at a time filled with the hapless soldiers on the beach, churning across the choppy waters of the Channel and returning for more. In the history of military rescues the moment stands out as an astonishment. All working together, the men did what individually could never have been done.

The fractures and chasms in our current national climate demonstrate the deepest of divisions. Red and Blue states, citizens and immigrants, and even uncertainty about who is really "male" and "female" divide and polarize our nation. Our current situation is a puzzle inside an enigma wrapped up in a puzzle. It may indeed be that World War II evidences the last time nearly everyone was united in a cause to save civilization for all. I have great concern regarding what would happen if our nation were confronted with the same call to unity today.

Yet whatever the nation may do, the Body of Christ must do. The mandate of biblical Christianity is "Bear one another's burdens" (Galatians 6:2). Whatever happens in divided America, in the Body of Christ we have no choice but to launch our little ships and help our brothers. When men do that, remarkable things happen. In my own beloved Texas, the Texans on Mission, a group of Baptist men, are always "on call" and ready to go to any disaster with trucks that feed thousands, trucks filled with washing machines for clothes, and teams to do everything from carrying off trees felled by tornadoes to cleaning up homes that are flooded. They are all in their own little boats showing up at a different kind of Dunkirk to help in the name of Christ.

In the same way that white blood cells surround impurities in the human body, implode them, and clean up messes in our physical bodies, even so men acting together can change lives that are surrounded by enemies and exposed to whatever happens. Just think of such organizations as Habitat for Humanity if you need your mind jogged. Together men can change everything in thousands of little Dunkirks. We look back on those days in 1940 with great nostalgia now. But we can also look forward to our own opportunities to launch our little lifeboats of help.

PAUSE TO PONDER
I Peter 4 :9-11

"Be hospitable to one another without complaint. [10] As each one has received a special gift, employ it in serving one another as good stewards of the multifaceted grace of God. [11] Whoever speaks is to do so as one who is speaking actual words of God; whoever serves is to do so as one who is serving by the strength which God supplies; so that in all things God may be glorified through Jesus Christ, to whom belongs the glory and dominion forever and ever. Amen."

MONDAY

Recall at least one impossible situation in your life when God intervened without any doubt. Thank Him and praise Him.

TUESDAY

Where are some Dunkirks in your school, job, neighborhood or city? What are some situations where folks are trapped and need intervention?

WEDNESDAY

Who do you know who could launch the boats and pick up someone stranded on a beach of impossibility? Could you put together a group of concerned men to do something for someone?

THURSDAY

Consider the limits of what you can do versus putting together groups of men to solve some wicked problem that one person cannot touch. Could you be a part of organizing men for a task that God has put on your heart?

FRIDAY

Celebrate with others the victory that is won when God acts in a specific situation and you are His partner in rescuing someone.

MARIS – NO ASTERISK IN GOD'S RECORD BOOK

"There is therefore now no condemnation for those who are in Christ Jesus" (ROMANS 8:1).

Roger Maris (1934-1985) had to live with an asterisk that is not there in the record books. On October 1, 1961, the New York Yankee Maris hit his 61st home run of the season against the Red Sox. That broke the 1927 record of the immortal Babe Ruth. The surly Midwestern man had never been as popular as the Babe. He had been in a contest with Mickey Mantle to break the record, but Mantle got hurt and Roger slugged on.

Immediately he got tattooed with an asterisk that never appeared in the record books. Baseball leaders complained that Babe Ruth's record was achieved in a 154- game season while Maris broke the record in the 159th game of the new 162-game American League season That is, Roger had five more chances to break the record. Hence the theoretical asterisk permanently glued to the record in many person's imaginations. His record was not broken until 1998, but most fans still remember his asterisk.

Eloquent intellectuals such as George Will and Doris Kearns Goodwin consider baseball a metaphor for life. Baseball and life are both individual and team endeavors. Thrilling victories and crushing defeats can happen in seconds. Defeat can be snatched from the jaws of victory. Unlike football and basketball, baseball is not played against any known clock. So also is life. We do not know how long we have when it begins. It may be cut short by rain or go into extra innings no one expected. So is baseball and life.

To the point, life leaves some of us with an asterisk. We did the best we could, but that was not enough for some folks. We planned, worked, and stayed in the game, but the way we did it, or how we did it, or when we did it stuck us with an asterisk. Indeed, almost no one gets out of life without an asterisk.

"He tried his best, but he was an alcoholic."
"She beat the odds, but she was married three times."
"He was successful, but he inherited the business from his father."
"She has a lot of friends, but her family disowned her."
And on and on and on. Stuck with an asterisk. What is yours?

Several times the Bible speaks of God's books. Most of us wonder what kind of asterisks may be on our page. If God keeps books, what kind of books does He keep? One thing is certain for the Christian. Once you ever confess that Jesus Christ is Lord and believe in your heart that God raised Him from the dead, there will never be another asterisk in God's books. He forgives fully, freely, finally, and forever. When you stand in His presence, you will not find an asterisk in His book. Your enemies, even some of your friends and family, may stick you with an asterisk. God does not. You will not be semi-saved, somewhat saved, or saved with some reservations. God will look at you as He looks at His own Son. When He looks at you, He will see Jesus. We are literally "in Christ."

You may argue that is too good to be true. That is why the gospel of Jesus Christ is good news. If all it did was leave you with an asterisk when you finally stand before God, what is the good of that news? You will not stand before God only to have Him say, "You are saved, but…." That is not salvation; that is disappointment. Either the blood of Jesus Christ saves us from all sin or not at all. That is why we sing with gusto, "There is wonder-working power in the blood." That is why Andre Crouch could write the words sung by thousands, "The blood will never lose its power."

Now, these are not promises to the man who mumbles a few words and then lives like the devil. Do not be fooled. God is not mocked. Just saying a pet phrase does not change things. What matters is something like this: "Lord, the only hope I have is you. I am throwing my life on you and your cross. I give you my life for the rest of my life. Rescue me from me right now; I have no other hope. I do not have a ghost of a chance of heaven other than your work on the cross. I do not deserve it and cannot earn it Lord, save me now." Any man who prays that and means it will never face a record book with an asterisk.

PAUSE TO PONDER
REVELATION 20 :12-15

"And I saw the dead, the great and the small, standing before the throne, and books were opened; and another book was opened, which is the book of life; and the dead were judged from the things which were written in the books, according to their deeds. [13] And the sea gave up the dead who were in it, and Death and Hades gave up the dead who were in them; and they were judged, each one of them according to their deeds.[14] Then Death and Hades were thrown into the lake of fire. This is the second death, the lake of fire. [15] And if anyone's name was not found written in the book of life, he was thrown into the lake of fire."

MONDAY

Get somewhere alone, look deeply into your own center, your
heart, and ask God to search it. Examine yourself and see
that you are really in the faith. If you feel you are not, pray
something like I wrote above right now. Don't wait. Do it.

TUESDAY

Give someone else a break. Stop the holier than the other
guy attitude, "Well, he's a pretty good guy BUT..." To use a
phrase: Butt out.

WEDNESDAY

Someone you know struggles with failure today.
Put an arm around them, encourage them, and let them
know God cares and forgives.

THURSDAY

When the devil drags up your past sins to torment you, point
him to the blood of the cross. Mock the devil. Stick his nose
in the blood of Jesus. Give him a bloody nose. The devil
gives you the only opportunity to cuss with the blessing of
God. Tell him where to go. He is already there anyway.

FRIDAY

Use this day to praise God for His unbelievable goodness and
kindness. Thank Him for the cross and the blood of Jesus.
Live like a man with no asterisk.

CHAPTER 37

LET IT RIP

Ripped jeans are denim jeans with tear or rips, often on the knees but possibly in other locations on the pants. They were popular in the late 1980s during the hard rock/heavy metal era and in the 1990s and 2000s during the grunge era. The punk culture also has been known to be fans of fabrics with various blemishes. But it was the uniform of the punk movement and later, grunge. At the time, it was a rebellious, anti-establishment statement. Then, torn jeans were a sign of rebellion but today—when everyone and his grandad are wearing them—it is more a sign of sheep-like conformism.

Ripped jeans are more expensive than their unmarred counterparts because that is fashionable to a certain demographic. However, getting your jeans aged and broken in just so is an artform in of itself.

The ripped shirt from the high-end fashion house Balmain costs $1,629. Holes in your wallet guaranteed also!

A pair of Maison Margiela trainers, complete with heavy distressing (multiple rips and tears) went on sale for $1,425.

For men of faith this may be one of the real off-the-wall, goofball, hard-to-consider trends. When I was a boy, you wore out the knees of your Levi's playing. It was no mark of distinction to have rips in your blue jeans. If I had told my mamma that I wanted an expensive pair of jeans because they were ripped, she would have made me go to my room and contemplate life for a few weeks. I cannot even think of what my dad would have thought. He might have sent me back to the farm to chop cotton for a year, with the suggestion I would next work on a Texas road crew.

For men of genuine faith, you can be who you are. You are not trying to look like someone you are not. Paul wrote the church in Turkey, "It is for freedom that Christ has set us free" (Galatians 5:1). For the sincere, sure enough grown-up Christian man, freedom means you do not have to be someone you are not. You are not ripping jeans or anything else to look a certain way. The psychologists talk about the difference between person and *persona*. The person is who you really are. The *persona* is who you are trying to look like. Old Karl Jung, one of the founders of psychiatry, sometimes spoke of our "shadow self." That is the opposite of our real self, which, outside of Christ and grace, we try to hide but cannot get rid of. When you come to Christ, you can drop every false façade, and for the first time in your life be who you really are created to be—a free man in Christ.

That means you no longer labor to impress others. You can just be who you are. The American image of the male species has changed over a century. The strong, silent western types—Doc Holiday or Wyatt Earp—exemplified a certain kind of manhood. They impressed with stony, steely-eyed silence. The Humphrey

Bogart type was a different kind of tough, as was the John Wayne type. What a difference in that view of manhood and the roles played by Tom Hanks, everybody's regular guy. Some men have tried on characters like trying on clothes. The freedom that Christ gives is the freedom to be you, without varnish or veneer. With Christ you can be the you God made you to be.

That means you do not have to get stuff to have a life. Payment for ripped up jeans may be the ultimate exposure of the silliness of just getting stuff. One businessman finally said, "I am tired of buying things I do not need to impress people I do not like."

Years ago, a man in Texas was buried in his Cadillac convertible, sitting at the wheel with the roof down. His grave was a huge hole large enough to bury the Cadillac. One of the mourners said out loud, "Man, that's living." No, it is not. I have been around some rich folks dying. Not one of them ever asked for more stuff at the end. They wanted their family and hoped they were ready to meet God.

That means you can limit regrets in your life. No man who walked on this planet will live and die free from regrets. It cannot be done. But you can limit regrets and leave here with far fewer if you find the freedom that Christ brings. All of us have done things with consequences that cannot be reversed. The good news of Jesus Christ is that any day, this very day, you can start afresh and live a life free of devastating regret.

You may not have ripped jeans, but outside of Jesus Christ you have something on the outside that hides the inside. You can be free of that.

"My brothers and sisters, do not hold your faith in our glorious Lord Jesus Christ with an attitude of personal favoritism. [2] For if a man comes into your assembly with a gold ring and is dressed in bright clothes, and a poor man in dirty clothes also comes in, [3] and you pay special attention to the one who is wearing the bright clothes, and say, "You sit here in a good place," and you say to the poor man, "You stand over there, or sit down by my footstool," [4] have you not made distinctions among yourselves, and become judges with evil motives? [5] Listen, my beloved brothers and sisters: did God not choose the poor of this world to be rich in faith and heirs of the kingdom which He promised to those who love Him? [6] But you have dishonored the poor man. Is it not the rich who oppress you and personally drag you into court? [7] Do they not blaspheme the good name by which you have been called? [8] If, however, you are fulfilling the royal law according to the Scripture, "You shall love your neighbor as yourself," you are doing well."

MONDAY

Ask yourself: What are the ripped jeans in your life?
What do you spend time and money on that does not reflect
who you really are on the inside? What can you rid
yourself of that is counterfeit?

TUESDAY

How are you trying to impress people in ways that do not
reflect who you are and what is in your center?

WEDNESDAY

Deliberately decide today to set aside something in your life
that is false, not true to the best you, and eliminate it.

THURSDAY

Ask a good friend to talk with you in a personal inventory
of your life. That is hard. It is tight but it is right.
Dare to ask someone close what seems real and what
seems like a veneer in your life.

FRIDAY

In a gentle way, help another man to shed something that
is not really him. In grace help someone free himself from
something. It might be a habit, stuff, or a relationship.
Help someone let go.

SPONTANEOUS ACTS
OF GOODNESS

Bill Murray is from an Irish Catholic family, the first of nine children. When asked about his faith, he is not reticent to reflect on what it means to him. Perhaps that is why his spontaneous acts have sparked such interest. Take this, for example.

Many of us have random impulses, but Bill Murray is the man who acts on them for all of us. Consider, for example, the time a couple of years ago when he caught a cab late at night in Oakland. Facing a long drive across the bay to Sausalito, he started talking with his cabbie and discovered that his driver was a frustrated saxophone player: He never had enough time to practice, because he was driving a taxi 14 hours a day. Murray told the cabbie to pull over and get his horn out of the trunk; the cabbie could play it in the back seat while Murray drove.

As he tells this story, Murray is sitting on a couch in a Toronto hotel. Wearing a rumpled shirt with purple stripes, he looks like he'd rather be playing golf than doing an interview. But his eyes light up as he remembers the sound of the cab's trunk opening: "This is gonna be a good one," he thought. Then he decided to "go all the way" and asked the back-seat saxophonist if he was hungry. The cabbie knew a great late-night BBQ place, but worried that it was in a sketchy neighborhood. "I was like, 'Relax, you got the horn,'" says Murray. So around 2:15 a.m., Bill Murray ate Oakland barbecue while his cab driver blew on the saxophone for an astonished crowd. "It was awesome," Murray says. "I think we'd all do that."

Many of us might do that if we were as famous as Billy Murray and like to use that fame in an unusual way. But you are not Bill Murray (unless you are reading this Bill, in which case I am Dennis Swanberg and would be pleased to allow you to do something for me). Most of us live quieter lives and anything spontaneous we would do would not grab headlines, on earth that is.

The Lord Jesus often did spontaneous acts of kindness. In fact, it was His way much of the time. When 5,000 were hungry, He fed them on the spot. When a wild man accosted Him at a cemetery, He fixed the wild man and made him whole. When He was on the way to raise the dead daughter of Jairus, there was a spontaneous moment inside a spontaneous moment. He healed the woman with the issue of blood on the way to raise the dead girl. If you look at His miracles, none of them were "planned" as we would use the word.

The Spirit of Christ will lead you to acts of spontaneous kindness if you are alert. When the electrician is working in 100-degree heat outside your house, give him some iced coffee. When the weary waiter looks so tired she cannot go another hour, leave her a 50% tip. When your pastor has had the hardest of weeks, send a travelling office masseur by for a backrub or take him to get a new suit. When the kid next door has his new bike stolen, get him another one. The list is really endless. Usually, it does not cost you anything. Most people just need somebody to listen to their stories. Find somebody and listen with empathy.

Now, spontaneity does not always work. A timid Christian homemaker read a book about spicing up her marriage. The book suggested that she wrap herself in Saran Wrap and greet her husband at the door with a rose in her mouth. When she opened the door, he fell into a chair and cried out, "My boss tried to fire me, I lost our best client, the IRS is going to audit us, I got a traffic ticket and now I come home to a drunk wife.'

There is always some risk in spontaneity, but the risk is worth the reward when lightening the load for someone. The famed preacher Charles H. Spurgeon visited his orphanage one day. He had built one of the largest orphanages in the world. A nurse took him to a little boy dying with tuberculosis. The preacher, who was as famous as Queen Victoria, asked the little boy if he wanted anything. The little boy said, "I have always wanted a bird in a cage." The great pastor, who could have ordered a dozen people to bring one, left immediately for the shops of south London, went door to door, got a bird in a cage from a shocked shopkeeper, and took it straight back to the little boy. A biographer who saw Spurgeon's entire life wrote, "This was his greatest moment." Suppose God said that about one spontaneous act of yours?

PAUSE TO PONDER
MARK 5 :25-34

"A woman who had had a hemorrhage for twelve years, [26] *and had endured much at the hands of many physicians, and had spent all that she had and was not helped at all, but instead had become worse—* [27] *after hearing about Jesus, she came up in the crowd behind Him and touched His cloak.* [28] *For she had been saying to herself, "If I just touch His garments, I will get well."* [29] *And immediately the flow of her blood was dried up; and she felt in her body that she was healed of her disease.* [30] *And immediately Jesus, perceiving in Himself that power from Him had gone out, turned around in the crowd and said, "Who touched My garments?"* [31] *And His disciples said to Him, "You see the crowd pressing in on You, and You say, 'Who touched Me?'"* [32] *And He looked around to see the woman who had done this.* [33] *But the woman, fearing and trembling, aware of what had happened to her, came and fell down before Him and told Him the whole truth.* [34] *And He said to her, "Daughter, your faith has made you well; go in peace and be cured of your disease."*

MONDAY

Review your own life and consider when you might have
spontaneous moments in your usual day.

TUESDAY

Capture a spontaneous moment when it presents itself. Risk
doing something in the moment that redeems the moment and
shows the love of Christ. Then, do not congratulate yourself.

WEDNESDAY

Use your influence to coordinate a spontaneous moment with
others for someone who needs to know others care. Ask the
Lord to show you what it is. Listen. He will.

THURSDAY

Look for something to do under your own roof or in your own
family that expresses a spontaneous goodness.

FRIDAY

Reflect on your attempts at spontaneity this week. Remember
the little scenes. Ask God to bless the people with the
memories of those moments.

SILENCE IS MORE THAN GOLDEN

Whoever belittles another lacks sense, but an intelligent person remains silent (**PROVERBS 11:12**).

The average person speaks about 7,000 words per day at a rate of 130 to 150 words per minute. That same typical human has a vocabulary of about 20,000 words. We are defined by our words. It may be true that people make up their minds about us in a second when they see our faces, but in the long run our words define us.

Even when we are trying to be funny, we may create outcomes we did not expect. Prior to a 1984 radio broadcast, Ronald Reagan was asked to speak into the microphone for a sound check. Joking, he said, "My fellow Americans, I'm pleased to tell you today that I've signed legislation that will outlaw Russia forever. We begin bombing in five minutes." A recording of his statement was leaked, and Soviet forces were briefly put on alert. On the other side of the aisle, who can forget the famously ambiguous statement of

Bill Clinton, "It depends on what the meaning of the word is is. If the—if he—if is means 'is and never has been,' that is not—that is one thing." Both elephants and donkeys are equally capable of making embarrassing statements.

It is like that Red Hot Chili Peppers' lyric, "Everyone has so much to say, they talk, talk, talk their lives away." When we are so intent on saying something, anything, on saying our piece, we miss the world passing us by.

I have mentioned Hawaiian Senator Daniel K. Inouye in another chapter, but want to use a different angle to his story. Another politician insulted the late Senator Inouye for using the wrong hand to shake hands. In the belittling statement, the politico said, "He doesn't even know how to shake hands with the proper hand." Here is what they did not know: Inouye volunteered to serve his country in June 1942, as soon as President Roosevelt decided to let Japanese Americans do so. Inouye was 18.

And in the Po Valley in Italy, as he was leading his platoon up a heavily defended hillside, a bullet hit him in the abdomen and came out his back. But Inouye kept going, advancing alone against a machine gun emplacement that had pinned down his men. He threw two grenades before his right arm was shattered by a German rifle grenade. But he kept going, switching to his left hand, painstakingly taking the grenade out of his unmovable and unusable right hand and throwing that grenade with his left hand. Then he advanced, firing his submachine gun, until another bullet blew him down the hillside. He was cited for the Medal of Honor and was awarded the Distinguished Service Cross, which was added to his Bronze Star, Purple Heart and 12 other medals and citations.

He gave his right arm for his country. It was amputated in Italy. After that, he asked to have a haircut, only to have a barber tell him, "I will not cut the hair of a Jap."

Both the critical politician and the barber were embarrassed into silence when they learned the truth about the brave Japanese American. He became a beloved United State Senator.

The wisest man in the world, who spoke most of the Proverbs, had a great deal to say about silence:

"When there are many words, transgression is unavoidable, but he who restrains his lips is wise" (PROVERBS 10:19).

"Even a fool, when he keeps silent, is considered wise. When he closes his lips, he is considered prudent" (PROVERBS 17:28).

"He who guards his mouth and his tongue guards his soul from troubles (PROVERBS 21:23)."

A wise man thinks before he talks. Someone said the tongue is so powerful that God put it behind two guards: your lips and your teeth. There is seldom a time when you can go wrong by saying nothing. There are a multitude of times when you ruin everything because you said something. That does not mean you have to become a Cistercian monk who does not say anything. It does mean you should measure your words before every response.

Just look at a group of men talking. I would dare you to find a man who speaks first and who speaks most who is considered the wisest person present by the other men. There is a holy restraint, a manly pause, and a considerate reticence that typifies the speech of a godly man. Sometimes the best thing to say is nothing.

PAUSE TO PONDER
PROVERBS 25 :11

"Like apples of gold in settings of silver,

Is a word spoken at the proper time."

MONDAY

Spend the day vigilant about your own speech in every situation:
on the phone with a client, waiting in line at the grocery store, and in
your own home. Observe when you speak and when you do not.

TUESDAY

Deliberately spend the day speaking as little as necessary.
This does not mean ignoring people or refusing necessary
knowledge. Just say as little as possible.
How did your day go?

WEDNESDAY

In a group speaking, deliberately decide to be the last
person to contribute. When you speak, do not say much.
Assess how you got heard.

THURSDAY

When you are tempted to sarcasm, belittling words, or snarky
speech, be quiet. Say nothing. Let it go.

FRIDAY

Ask a trusted friend what he thinks about your speech, silences,
and words. Get a real assessment.

CHAPTER 40

FIELD OF BEANS

"Field of Dreams" remains an American treasure, even though it was released in 1989. Ray Kinsella lives with his wife, Annie, and daughter, Karin, on their Iowa corn farm. He is troubled by the relationship with his late father, John Kinsella, a devoted baseball fan. Kevin Costner will forever be remembered for this movie. It was nominated for three Academy Awards, including best picture.

Walking through his cornfield one evening, Ray hears a voice whispering, "If you build it, he will come", and sees a vision of a baseball diamond in his field and the great Shoeless Joe Jackson. Ray figures that if he builds a baseball field, Shoeless Joe, whom his father idolized, can play baseball again. Annie is skeptical but agrees to him plowing part of the corn to build a baseball field, despite the financial loss. Spoiler alert. If you are one of few folks who do not know the plot, get the movie.

In the history of God's people, there is the story not of a "Field of Dreams" but of a "Field of Beans." It only takes two verses:

Next to him was Shammah son of Agee, the Hararite. The Philistines gathered together at Lehi, where there was a plot of ground full of lentils; and the army fled from the Philistines. But he took his stand in the middle of the plot, defended, and killed the Philistines; and the Lord brought about a great victory (2 SAMUEL 23:11-12).

These two verses belong to list of the deeds of King David's "Mighty Men," as they are called. Mighty Man Abishai took out 300 enemies with his own spear. Benaiah killed a lion in the bottom of a pit in the winter. Those two guys had marquee quality he-man victories, dramatic exploits of the first variety. Compared to that, Shammah does not come off looking like a super-hero. He took his stand in a field of beans. When his comrades in arms, the Israeli army, fled the bean field, Shammah stayed, fought, and defended the field of beans. Most of us would agree that a field of beans is not a field of dreams. It is far more dramatic to kill a lion or 300 men with one spear than defending a field of beans.

Beans don't get much respect. When someone stretches the truth, we say, "He is full of beans." When we do not like the accounting department, we call them "bean counters." When college kids cannot afford a chair, they get a bean bag chair. When something has no known value, we say, "That isn't worth a hill of beans." Beans just don't get much respect. Yet Shammah got his name in the Bible, which is more than you and I will get, because he was faithful to defend a field of beans from God's enemies. Right there with David, Solomon, Isaiah, the Lord Jesus, Peter, and Paul, in the same book, we read the name Shammah. He defended a field of beans.

He did not discount what God gave him to do compared with others. I expect Shammah would rather have had the notoriety of being a lion killer or something else dramatic. Not everyone can be a lion killer. Most of those among David's Mighty Men did something dramatic, brave, and astounding. Shammah defended a field of beans. Yet that field belonged to the Promised Land. That was the land promised to Abraham a thousand years before. Every square foot of it was part of the covenant of God. It was Shammah's legacy and patrimony. He would not give up an inch of the Holy Land to the godless Philistines. It was not dramatic, but it was his assignment.

Most of us will lead quiet lives, not that of marquee players. If you are a *Gone with the Wind* fan, we will be more like Ashley than Rhett, more like Melanie than Scarlet. We will have lives of quiet faithfulness. As a pastor for years, I can tell you without reservation that the church of the risen Christ is not built by daredevils who are Christian Evel Knievel's. The church stays alive because of quiet folks who take care of the little corner that God gave them and are faithful over little. If God has given you a field of beans, stand faithful in that field. He does not expect you to build pyramids if He has given you pebbles, but He expects you to build something.

He refused to give up what belonged to God. There comes a moment in every man's life when he must draw a line. The man who refuses to draw a line anywhere is not worthy of the Kingdom of God. There is a moment that marks your life, when you take a stand and say, "No further." You do not have to be mean, angry, or hateful to draw a line, but draw a line you must someday. When everyone else fled, Shammah would not give up to the enemies of God's people a field of beans that belonged to the Holy Land. He did not give an inch.

God's estimate of greatness is not ours. For thousands of years, first Jews and now also Christians have read this tiny story. People who never heard of Michael Jordan, Tom Brady, or Lady Gaga have read of Shammah, and when future people know none of those names, millions will read about Shammah for another thousand years. With God you are great if you are faithful over the patch of life He gave you.

PAUSE TO PONDER
III John 1 :1-6

"The elder to the beloved Gaius, whom I love in truth.

2 Beloved, I pray that in all respects you may prosper and be in good health, just as your soul prospers. 3 For I was overjoyed when brothers came and testified to your truth, that is, how you are walking in truth. 4 I have no greater joy than this, to hear of my children walking in the truth.

5 Beloved, you are acting faithfully in whatever you accomplish for the brothers and sisters, and especially when they are strangers; 6 and they have testified to your love before the church. You will do well to send them on their way in a manner worthy of God."

MONDAY

What is your field of beans? This is a metaphor, a way of
speaking, and a symbol. God has given you a patch of
something to stand in and hold.

TUESDAY

Do you compare yourself to others in the assignments that
God has given you? Do you feel less than or more than
others because of the corner God handed to you?
Do not compare His assignments to you with his
assignments to others.

WEDNESDAY

Where do you draw the line with the enemies of God? Drug
dealers, porno purveyors, abortionists, and an army
of Philistines want to take you. your family, and your life.
Take a stand somewhere.

THURSDAY

If you do not know what your field is, ask God. Ask Him
persistently, daily, and He will show you where your field is.
Take it and defend it.

FRIDAY

Help someone else who believes his field is not important,
his patch is not worth defending. Sometimes you must put
some steel in your brother's backbone.
Do it with tough love.

CHAPTER 41

ODD FOR GOD

Are you willing to be odd for God? Are you willing to be a joke at the office, different from your godless neighbors in the neighborhood, or a standout in your dormitory? God often calls His people to be odd for him. In the movie *Greyhound*, Tom Hanks plays the commander of a convoy protecting U.S. naval ships, who prays before every meal, while the profane young men who report to him look at him as if he is some kind of freak. He was willing to be odd for God. Adapted from E. M. Forrester's 1955 work, "The Good Shepherd," the movie follows Captain Ernie Krause on his February 1942 maiden voyage as commander of the *USS Keeling*, the destroyer from whose codename the picture takes its title. His is one of three such vessels protecting a convoy of troop transports and supply ships crossing the North Atlantic to the U.K.

The action centers on the period of five days during which the convoy must pass through an area of the ocean beyond the reach of Allied air support. This exposes it to the marauding of a wolfpack of German U boats.

Krause's Christian faith is prominent in Hanks' script. In fact, the first scene in which he features, finds him praying on his knees.

Krause has a particular fondness for the verse from the Letter to the Hebrews, which proclaims that "Jesus Christ is the same yesterday, today and forever" (Hebrews 13:8).

In the brief flashback to December 1941 that constitutes the film's minimal but effective romantic interlude, Krause gives a Christmas ornament with those words inscribed on it to his girlfriend, Evelyn (Elizabeth Shue).

Krause's beliefs provide him with the firm foundation and far-reaching perspective he will need as, with the aid of his executive officer, Charlie Cole (Stephen Graham), he battles enemy submarines and maneuvers through heavy seas. Under the pressure of apparently overwhelming challenges, his humane values and ability to endure endless hours at the helm come to the fore.

As might be expected, Krause's vocabulary does not include the kind of words proverbially associated with sailors. In fact, when another character drops the dialogue's lone F-bomb, it goes off with an unusually percussive effect. The movie underscores the power of a man willing to be odd for God, different from the other sailors on the ship.

Such prophets as Ezekiel (12:1-6) were willing to be odd for God, different for the divine, and considered looney for the Lord. In that passage, God told Ezekiel to dress like a street person and look as if he were leaving town through digging a hole in the wall.

His generation called him nuts. History calls him a major prophet.

Tom Hanks' character and Ezekiel remind men today that there is a price to pay in ridicule and rejection when you are odd for God. At the end of the movie, however, the profane young sailors respect Hanks' character, even if they do not understand him. In our godless and secular generation, men who stand up for the right to life, reject the redefinition of the family, oppose gay marriage, and refuse to honor the pornographic are an oddity. Yet that is the call of the Christ. You may be mocked at the university, rejected at work, eat alone while colleagues tell their profane stories, and find yourself the object of mockery. Yet that is the call of the Christ. Earlier generations of Christians understood there is a price to pay for following Jesus. The great hymn by Isaac Watts says,

> Am I a soldier of the cross,
> a follower of the Lamb,
> and shall I fear to own his cause,
> or blush to speak his name?
>
> Must I be carried to the skies
> on flowery beds of ease,
> while others fought to win the prize,
> and sailed through bloody seas?
>
> Are there no foes for me to face?
> Must I not stem the flood?
> Is this vile world a friend to grace,
> to help me on to God?

Today Isaac Watts is honored all over the world. That was not the case in his life. He was buried in Bunhill Fields in London when he died. That was the place religious dissenters were buried. They could not be buried where the elite Anglicans were buried. They were buried in a place of scorn. Today we honor those who were rejected in their day as odd for God.

PAUSE TO PONDER
MATTHEW 3 :1-6

"Now in those days John the Baptist came, preaching in the wilderness of Judea, saying, [2] "Repent, for the kingdom of heaven is at hand." [3] For this is the one referred to by Isaiah the prophet when he said,

"The voice of one calling out in the wilderness,
'Prepare the way of the Lord,
Make His paths straight!'"

[4] Now John himself had a garment of camel's hair and a leather belt around his waist; and his food was locusts and wild honey. [5] At that time Jerusalem was going out to him, and all Judea and all the region around the Jordan; [6] and they were being baptized by him in the Jordan River, as they confessed their sins."

MONDAY

Take an honest inventory of your life. Where do you stand out as different from the secular people around you, and do so openly?

TUESDAY

Determine where and when you will be odd for God in your own life: a place, an issue, a moment in time.

WEDNESDAY

Ask God today to give you the courage to be odd for God.

THURSDAY

Make this the day to take your stand. Do not laugh at the profane or pretend you are "one of gang" when God is mocked.

FRIDAY

Find someone else and stand with him as he does the same.

SHADED JOY –
ENJOYING THE MISFORTUNE
OF ANOTHER MAN

The Swan studied Greek at Baylor. There was a saying that "the Greeks have a word for everything." It is a rich language, not the least because it is the language of the Bible. It is not alone in having interesting compound words. There is a German word, Schadenfreude. Do not worry about saying it. It combines two words: one for *shade* and the other for *joy*. It means joy that is in the shade. What it refers to is one of the uglier aspects of human life: rejoicing in the misfortune of another person. Your grouchy neighbor with an ugly yard gets fined by the city for not mowing his grass. Your hateful sister-in-law loses her job. The smart-aleck in the office gets demoted. All of these are occasions for rejoicing in the misfortune of another person. You get the idea.

This is off limits for godly people. In the Old Testament, the neighbors of Israel rejoiced in her destruction by the Babylonians

(Iraqis) 500 years before Christ. Their neighbors celebrated the fall of God's people. The Ammorites held a dance. The Moabites made snarky remarks. The Edomites kicked them when they were down. The Philistines jumped on them after the Edomites (Ezekiel 25:1-17). These neighbors who surrounded Israel like the numbers on a clockface all rejoiced in her misfortune. The response of God was to be unsparing in His judgment of these people. They would basically disappear from history.

We do not think of rejoicing in the misfortune of others as much of a sin. God does. He acts against those who do it. We see murder, adultery, grand theft, and stuff like that as obnoxious to God. God Himself sees it as obnoxious when we rejoice in the loss and hurt of someone else, especially His own people. There is nowhere this is truer than in His church. Churches as a whole of individuals in a local church sometimes play the game of "gotcha." A church in the suburbs where tens of thousands of people are moving boom and an older church in an urban area loses its members to the new church. Then the new church gets into trouble – they cannot pay the mortgage, or the pastor embarrasses the church. What is the attitude of the folks in the church struggling downtown? All too many times, the attitude has been one of not-so-concealed rejoicing.

This happens in offices and families. The bright new whiz kid with an Ivy League degree makes partner in a shorter time than a whole gang of people who have toiled away for years. Then he loses a client, or she flubs a case. How do the others in the office react?

This can also happen in families. One sibling toils away for years at the same job and barely has enough to retire. Another sibling marries a drunk, they live an irresponsible life, and then the drunk inherits a fortune and they live in a beautiful house overlooking an astonishing body of water. What is the attitude of the drudge who worked so hard and has nothing? This is the real stuff that can poison life, ruin health, embitter spirits, and create a toxic atmosphere.

If God judged shaded joy among pagan nations addressed by Ezekiel 2500 years ago, He must surely judge that attitude among those who claim to follow the Lord Jesus Christ. Indeed, the Christian attitude of love fixes its mind on "whatever is true, whatever is honorable, whatever is just, whatever is pure, whatever is pleasing, whatever is commendable; if there is any excellence, and if there is anything worthy of praise, think about these things" (Philippians 4:8). This eliminates all celebration of the bad fortune of other people.

Do you know what will help you deal with the temptation to gloat over the misfortune of others? I can give you a simple suggestion. Just think of what would have happened to you if everything you have ever done or thought that was not worthy, publicly caught up with you. Unless you are so sanctified you are already an angel, you have said and done things that would have shattered your life if they caught up with you. By the grace of God, you have avoided what might have been revealed, you have dodged what might have been exposed, and you have been spared from what everyone might have known.

Only by the grace of God has stuff not caught up with you.

If you dwell on that fact with gratitude, it will become a strong remedy against rejoicing in the cownfall of others. If you thank God for his protection in your life from the outcomes you really deserved, it will insulate you from rejoicing in the hard times of others. There is no better safeguard against shaded joy.

Beyond that, Jesus called the hand of folks who came to Him pointing out the fall of others. Some told him about others, some folks came to Him with the latest on Fox or CNN: Some Galileans had been slaughtered by Pilate and a tower in Jerusalem fell on 18 people (Luke 13:1-5). Jesus gave them a strong warning. Rather than gloat over the fact they were still alive, these gossips should repent themselves. When we hear of the downfall of others, our response should be personal repentance, not gloating. That pleases God and it will make you a ton happier than shaded joy.

PAUSE TO PONDER
PHILIPPIANS 4 :8-9

"Finally, brothers and sisters, whatever is true, whatever is honorable, whatever is right, whatever is pure, whatever is lovely, whatever is commendable, if there is any excellence and if anything worthy of praise, think about these things. [9] As for the things you have learned and received and heard and seen in me, practice these things, and the God of peace will be with you."

MONDAY

When you get word about ill fate happening to someone you
do not care for, pray for them, and ask God to
give you empathy.

TUESDAY

Rather than gloat over someone's misfortune around you, give
them a word of encouragement and genuine sympathy.

WEDNESDAY

Make an actual list of the things in your life that would have
hurt you had they been known, but by the grace of God that
did not happen. Dwell on that in gratitude.

THURSDAY

Read Philippians 4 several times today. Think about these
things…"whatsoever things are honest, whatsoever things are
just, whatsoever things are pure, whatsoever things are of good
report. Do I exemplify these virtues in my life?

FRIDAY

When someone else is gloating over the misfortune
of another person, inject a positive and redemptive note
into the conversation.

WARNING LABELS

I remember my Dad, Floyd, coming home to watch the network news in the 60's and 70's. In those days, fathers came home from work, sat down in a recliner, and turned on the 5:30 p.m. news. Some listened to Uncle Walter Cronkite and some to Huntley and Brinkley. Some of you know who I am talking about. Others of you are more familiar with Hobbits than those names. Whatever.

My point is, today I am like my dad. I turn on the network news and listen to Lester. Sometimes it's just good to listen to news where everybody isn't talking at one time and screaming at one another. Don't get me wrong; I listen to a certain cable news channel, but after a long day of travel I just like to listen to someone calm, even if I do not agree with them. There is something different, however, about the network news nowadays. It is filled with pharmaceutical commercials because folks like me with cholesterol or bad knees or sleep apnea or something else buy drugs. I am always amused on TV and radio when a drug commercial ends with an auctioneer saying something like:

Use of Wonder Drug may cause coma, loss of all hair, loss of fingernails and toenails, loss of teeth, loss of vision, hearing, tasting, smelling, and your mind. Some users have had strokes, heart attacks, leprosy, anemia, and hang nails. If your eyes do not blink for two days after taking Wonder Drug, please see your doctor immediately.

You know what I mean. The cure seems worse than what it is supposed to heal.

Yet we do need warning labels. A friend of mine collects some of them. My all-time favorite is this one on a bag of peanuts: "Beware. This bag contains nuts." You would have to be nuts not to know that the bag contains nuts. It makes me nuts even to read that.

Wouldn't it be good if life itself came with warning labels? Warning: Stop surfing the internet at midnight looking for stuff you wouldn't want your wife or mother to see. Warning: Stop dropping by the bar for just one drink. Warning: Stop reporting personal purchases on your expense report. Warning: Stop taking your secretary to three-hour lunches. Warning: Stop working so late you miss your son's ballgame. Warning: Stop leaving your Bible on your dashboard until next Sunday. You get the idea.

Yet your life does have warning labels. They are throughout the Bible. Look at every command that God gave you and it is a warning label. Warning: Flee immorality. The Bible does not say pray about it, think it over, ponder it, wait for a special sign, or do what your neighbor does. The warning label says: FLEE. What part of that do you not understand? You cannot take fire into your bosom and not be burned. There is something simple about a good pair of Nikes or Adidas. Just FLEE.

Or take Paul's warning label to Timothy: Seek righteousness. If it is right, holy, good, wholesome, pursue it like a hunter pursuing deer, like a beaver looking for a log, like a salmon trying to get back where it started. With passion, seek what is right, positive, edifying, uplifting, and good. In this weary, old, sinful world, righteousness does not pursue you. The devil chases you. Lust stalks you. Greed ambushes you. You must pursue righteousness. Chase it. Run after it. As I've said before, use that Nike theology: Just Do It.

God Himself often puts warning labels right in front of you. The Word says, "You will not be tempted beyond what you are able to resist. God will with temptation make a way of escape" (1 Corinthians 10:13). If you look at the times you have tripped, fallen, and broken yourself into pieces, you will always discover there was a way out…always. You are about to go where you should not go, and the phone rings with a cheery voice from a Christian friend. You are about to meet who you are not supposed to meet, and Charles Stanley (In Touch), David Jeremiah (Turning Point or Robert Jeffress (Pathways to Victory) shows up on the radio at just that moment. You are about to take what you are not supposed to take, and right there on your desk is a copy of My Utmost for His Highest. Think about it. God sends warning labels all the time. You must shut your eyes and close your ears not to see them and hear them. Look for the labels.

Warning labels are usually very simple. On the hairdryer the label reads: "Do not use while in water." Duh. On the microwave the label warns: "Do not dry your pet's hair in the microwave." That is deep. Warning labels are usually clear, short, and not mistakable. That is the way God's warning labels are as well. They are clear, short, and easy to understand. Adam and Eve got a very short warning: Do not eat anything on that tree. How hard is that?

Look for the labels. They are always there right in front of you.

PAUSE TO PONDER
I Timothy 6 :11-16

*"But flee from these things, you man of God, and pursue righteousness, godliness, faith, love, perseverance, and gentleness. 12 Fight the good fight of faith; take hold of the eternal life to which you were called, and for which you made the good confession in the presence of many witnesses. 13 I direct you in the presence of God, who gives life to all things, and of Christ Jesus, who testified the good confession before Pontius Pilate, 14 that you keep the commandment without fault **or** reproach until the appearing of our Lord Jesus Christ, 15 which He will bring about at the proper time—He who is the blessed and only Sovereign, the King of kings and Lord of lords, 16 who alone possesses immortality and dwells in unapproachable light, whom no one has seen or can see. To Him be honor and eternal dominion! Amen."*

MONDAY

Think of the times God clearly put a warning label in front of you. Did you read it or ignore it? What was the consequence?

TUESDAY

Sometimes you have to be the warning label for another man. You do not have to be ugly, make a long speech, or put somebody down. You just need to say at the right moment, "Watch out."

WEDNESDAY

Spend today on the lookout for one warning label from God. It could be a news story, or what happened to a co-worker who threw everything away, or just a quiet uneasiness in your own conscience. Read the labels.

THURSDAY

Read the Ten Commandments. Read them again. Ask God which of His Big Ten are a warning label to you right now. He will tell you.

FRIDAY

Read 1 Timothy 6. Circle every word in that chapter that warns you, urges caution, or otherwise tells you what is wise to do.

UNBREAKABLE –
THE WINDOW CAN BREAK

By now it is a byword, a joke, an unforgettable moment in bad marketing. Elon Musk intended to unveil his Cybertruck in the most dramatic way possible. After taking a sledgehammer to the body, an engineer then threw metal balls at the windows that could not be broken. The problem was that before Elon, the audience, and now the whole world, both the unbreakable windows broke. It may have been the most ridiculous product unveiling in the history of reveals.

Musk quickly explained what had gone wrong, but the damage had been done and the memory remained. Move over Titanic, the unbreakable ship. Alongside that disaster, on a lower, lighter level is the Elon Musk Cybertruck disaster. Be very careful when you proclaim before God and all the world that something is unsinkable or unbreakable. It might just sink or break. The Apostle Paul had just that thing in mind when he wrote 1 Corinthians 10:12, "So, if you think you are standing firm, be careful that you do not fall."

This is more than the tried and true maxims, "The bigger they are the harder they fall." It is even different than the warning to the CEO, "The higher a monkey climbs up a tree, the more he shows his rear end." It is more akin to the proverb, "Pride comes before the fall" (Proverbs 16:18). There is a spiritual reality about complacent confidence that does not put God into the equation. The Bible and church history demonstrate clearly no one is above anything absent the grace of God. The first murder took place after a worship service and was a fratricide. Noah preached righteousness, saved his family in the ark, and then got so drunk he didn't know he was naked. Moses got mad at a rock and ruined his own future. David slept with Uriah's wife and killed Uriah after he wrote the 23rd Psalm. Peter promised he would die for Jesus, only to cuss that he did not even know him the same night he bragged about his steadfastness. In two of his letters Paul considered Demas to be a faithful fellow-worker, only finally to state sadly that Demas forsook him because he loved the visible world of the now. And on and on. When famous evangelists stay true to the cause, members of their own family may fall. Beloved pastors who were trusted mentors fall and discourage multitudes.

Write this down. Say it out loud right now: "I am capable of anything apart from the sustaining grace of God and constant fellowship with Him." Your flesh is unimproved and unimprovable. When you come to God through Christ you get a new life. You have available the power of God in the indwelling Holy Spirit, but your flesh never improves. The flesh of a 100-year-old Christian is just as wicked as the flesh of an infant in Christ. Only the power of God can keep you from anything. When you read the front page of the paper and discover murder, adultery, embezzlement, corruption, and everything else on the front page, it is only the grace of that it is not your picture there. Nearby cities have provided many an illustration of doing things "on the road" (while away from home) that were revealed on the 6 o'clock news and the morning newspaper and the social media outlets. Some pharisaical Christians laugh under their breath, but an honest man should thank God that, without His grace, he could have been plastered across the front page to the shame of his family and church. You are capable of anything apart from the grace and power of God. Elon Musk thought his Cybertruck windows could withstand a steel ball. They cracked at the first assault and so will you without the power of God.

In my book *No More Secrets*, I shared the story of a devout abbot in charge of a monastery. There were rumors that a new monk was smuggling a woman into his cell and indulging in the weakness of the flesh. The suspicious monks demanded the abbot take a group of them to the young monk's cell. The wise abbot took a group to the cell and surprised the young monk. The abbot saw a barrel next to the bed in the sparse cell. He sat down on top of the barrel. He told the other monks to search the simple cell. They looked high and low, under the bed and in the corners. There was no woman there. The abbot rebuked them for their suspicion and sent them away. When they were gone, he got off the barrel. Both he and the novice knew who was in the barrel. The old abbot told the novice, "Go, and sin no more." The young monk never forgot the abbot who sat on the barrel.

How many times in your life has God sat on the barrel?

PAUSE TO PONDER
JUDE 24

"Now to Him who is able to protect you from stumbling,

and to make you stand in the presence of His glory,

blameless with great joy."

MONDAY

Identify the areas in your life where you are certain you could never fall. List them. Meditate on that list. Remind yourself that you could fall for any one of them at any time without God.

TUESDAY

Review the stories of those Bible characters who fell. Get acquainted with Samson, the sons of Eli, and Judas, as well as those mentioned above. Consider in humility that you are no better than they were.

WEDNESDAY

Start the day with the confession to God that you are weak, destitute of power, and needy without the power of God in your life. Meditate on the Cross of Christ and what your sin cost Him.

THURSDAY

Have you already fallen this week? Have you looked where you should not look, lingered where you should have run away, or said what you should not have said? Confess it to God and call out for His cleansing.

FRIDAY

Find an accountability partner you can trust. Talk and pray with that other man, a mature Christian. Pledge to tell him the truth and ask for prayer.

NO CARDBOARD FANS

Major league baseball was founded in 1869. America's game has witnessed and weathered wars, the Depression, its own scandals, shattering cultural changes, a major strike, and even recently a pandemic that shortened its season to 60 games played in empty stadiums. Something utterly new in the storied history of baseball is rare.

The rare has now happened. I was watching the summer camp game between the Mets and the Yankees when I saw it with my own eyes. There were cardboard fans, cut-out devotees, sitting in the stands. Some teams are offering their fans the opportunity to have their cardboard image propped up in the stadium in 2020. The sightless, silent pieces of paper stare with unseeing eyes at the MLB games. Added to that, the league is piping in recorded crowd noise to keep the situation from being eerily silent. They crank the noise up on a double play and let it scream when there is a home run.

You have to wonder how this all actually motivates the millionaires playing a boy's game in an empty, silent stadium. Does the presence and affirmation of fans actually mean that much? Wouldn't the knowledge that a million folks are watching on TV not motivate them? What is actually in the head of Mike Trout with his 12-year $426.5 million contract when he sees a paper fan and hears recorded cheers? Who knows?

Hebrews 12:1 reminds the believer that "we are surrounded by so great a cloud of witnesses." The writer puts you in the floor of a great Roman arena. Above you and around you row-upon-row are those faithful believers who have gone before you. They are at rest above; you are still in the game below. Hebrews calls them "witnesses." That does not so much mean they are watching your life as it means they are calling out from the stands that you can finish the game strong. All of the names in Hebrews 11, Abel and Abraham, Moses and Joseph, plus all the godly folks who helped to raise you and who are now in the life beyond, are witnessing to you that you too can finish strong in the arena of faith. Their lives are not cardboard cutouts but are living souls who have gone before you and are now in the presence of God awaiting your joining them in the not-too-distant future. "He is not the God of the dead but of the living" (Mark 12:27).

In the early church, there was a much greater sense that we are living the Christian life in our own day under the testimony of those who have gone before us. This is not spooky or bizarre; it is a real aspect of the Christian faith. Those of us still below are the church militant. We are still in the battle. Those who are at rest are in the church triumphant, the church at rest. These are not paper fans. They are real unseen presences that spur us on to finish well in our own day. By their name and stories, they witness to you that faith can endure, and you can finish with triumph. The skies are not empty. They are filled with the spirits of the just made perfect (Hebrews 12:23).

Sometimes in the Christian life you have to encourage yourself. A great Christian coach I know led his university to win the most spectacular game in its history. The game is still recalled a half-century later. Yet the university did not give him a bonus or gift for the triumph. He went out and bought himself a gold Rolex and had it engraved to congratulate himself. He still wears it decades later with the inscription made by himself for himself. Sometimes you have to talk to yourself, encourage yourself, and edify yourself. You can say, "Self, you can stay faithful even in this." Encouraging self-talk is important.

Other believers may encourage you. We are commanded to "encourage one another and build one another up" (1 Thessalonians 5:11). You can be sure that everyone you meet needs encouraging. Do not exempt anyone. Some of the most "successful" people you meet need encouragement from you. You would be surprised who around you needs encouragement. You never waste affirmation of another.

Yet at the highest level, you need to remember those who have gone before you. When I think of the folks who encouraged me at Baylor, Southwestern Seminary, and church members who have now joined the Church at rest in Heaven above, they are among the highest of all encouragers. There is an old hymn from 1906

that we used to sing that reminds us of those who have trusted us
to carry on:

> I would be true, for there are those who trust me;
> I would be pure, for there are those who care;
> I would be strong, for there is much to suffer;
> I would be brave, for there is much to dare.

PAUSE TO PONDER
Hebrews 12 :1

"Therefore, since we also have such a great cloud of witnesses surrounding us, let's rid ourselves of every obstacle and the sin which so easily entangles us, and let's run with endurance the race that is set before us."

MONDAY

Reflect today on those mentors who have gone on and are
in heaven's grandstands. Ask yourself how each of them
influenced you and how your life today would please them.

TUESDAY

Spend this day in conscious reflection on the characters in
Hebrews 11, those great biblical heroes in the grandstands of
heaven. How do their lives encourage you? They were not
perfect, but they finished well.

WEDNESDAY

Today remember the name and face and testimony of that
person who influenced you the most. If they could speak to you
directly today, what would they say to encourage your faith?

THURSDAY

Pull out an old church directory, college annual, or other
source of pictures such as google images and find the picture
of someone who believed in you, challenged you, and
encouraged you. Keep that image through the day.

FRIDAY

Come alongside a friend and engage them to name the person
who influenced them most. Talk about it.

LITTLE THINGS THAT
KEEP ON AT IT

Four things on earth are small, yet they are exceedingly wise (**PROVERBS 30:24**).

The wisest man who ever lived must have been a close observer of nature. He focuses on ants, badgers, locusts, and lizards.

The context of Proverbs 30:24-28 is about the resilience of creatures with seeming disadvantages. The ants overcome their weakness by planning well for the future (30:25), the badgers overcome their feebleness by living in well protected areas (30:26), and the locusts overcome the lack of an order-giving leader by every individual carrying out its own responsibility (30:27). In this context, the spider, though small, overcomes its seeming insignificance by using its hands to make its home in kings' palaces (30:28).

God made visible creation to teach us about invisible truths (Romans 1:20). When we look at the wonders of nature, they point to the wisdom of God. I know some academics and philosophers want you to think that everything you see is a cosmic accident. From the gopher to the galaxy, from the monkey to the Milky Way, it is just an accident in a universe with no God. If you believe that, you think a printing plant could grow up and unabridged dictionaries would fall out of the air! God made all things wise and wonderful, all things great and small. And He is the Lord God of all.

The ant lives in a world with a division of labor. With remarkable tenacity the ant prepares for the future. Badgers protect themselves by living in inaccessible places. Locusts move in mass as if in an organized army. Of greatest interest to me is the spider. The wise man indicates this tiny bug cannot be kept out of the king's palace. Augustus with his empire, Napoleon with his personal guard, Bill Gates with his security system on Lake Washington, or the President of the United States cannot keep a spider out of their residences. With perseverance and mystery, the spider makes a way inside. The biblical prophet Zechariah put it this way: "Who dares despise the day of small thing?" (4:10). We live in a world that worships the big, honors the large, and covets the huge. Yet God can use small things, and usually does.

When Fred Smith proposed what would become FedEx in a thesis for his Harvard MBA, they gave him a "C" and told him it was crazy to take on the Post Office. John Grisham could not get a publisher for his first book, so he sold A Time to Kill out of the trunk of his car. A young man with no job sold used cheese out of a handcart. His name was Kraft. Facebook started in a dorm room. YouTube started in a cubicle. Apple and Google started in some dudes' garages. Walt Disney started it all in an apartment. Jeff Bezos shipped books out of his garage. Mattel was started by two Polish immigrants who thought it would be cute to sell Teddy Bears, named after Teddy Roosevelt. Nearly nothing starts big.

This is emphatically true of the work of the Lord Jesus Christ. He said His Kingdom was the size of a mustard seed when it began (Mark 4:30-32). Look at it. He lived in a tiny country the size of New Jersey. Israel was an occupied country and oppressed. His followers were unknown working men and despised rejects. He never went more than 120 miles from his hometown. His miracles happened in tiny towns named Cana and Bethany. Yet today more than 70,000 people will call Him Lord for the first time and His Kingdom circles the earth. Nothing ever got bigger that started so small. What does all of this mean for you?

Most things stop because they never start. Men have big ideas, great schemes, and grand plans. But nothing happens. Why? It is because they do not do the first things. At the University of Texas commencement speech in 2014, Admiral William McRaven became famous by telling the privileged graduates that the most important thing they could do in the morning was to get up and make their bed. The speech echoed around the world. Do something to start. Too many lives are like the Unfinished Symphony. Start something small.

Too many men want BIG immediately and despise little. Jesus did not begin with big stuff. He started with unknown fishermen mending nets and a jerk named Matthew who ripped off the taxpayers. Jesus started small and gave the beginning to the

Father. He did not start with a worldwide church. He started with a handful of dull disciples who did not even understand His most basic teachings.

Are you more spiritual than Jesus? Start with what you have. The Salvation Army circles the world today. Yet William Booth was an unemployed father of six children with no education and no future when he started it in East London. People emptied chamber pots full of excrement on him and threw rotten eggs at him. He kept on marching, and look at it today. Start small and give it to God. Let Him be in charge of BIG.

PAUSE TO PONDER
Luke 1 :49-50

"For the Mighty One has done great things for me;

And holy is His name.

[50] *And His mercy is to generation after generation*

Toward those who fear Him."

MONDAY

Start this week by doing something small that you have
intended to do. Clean up your desk. Take the papers there
and file them, refer them or trash them. Get out of the
paralysis of analysis.

TUESDAY

Reflect on the successful people and projects you know about.
How many of them started small? All of them.
Think small today.

WEDNESDAY

Start something today by taking one step on a project.
If you want to build something, order a blueprint. If you want
to learn to cook a great omelet, buy a pan and crack the eggs.
If you want to read a biography, open the book and read a page.
Most of all, if you want to read the Bible read one chapter this
morning. Just do it.

THURSDAY

Give someone something small today that could make a
difference. Give a front-line worker a double tip and bless her.

FRIDAY

Help somebody wrestling with something small. Lift a box,
carry a load, or pick up an item and help somebody
struggling with small.

CHAPTER 47

POWER PLANT

Outside Muleshoe, Texas, in the remote area of the Texas Panhandle, there is an enormous coal-fired electrical power plant. Long railroad trains with scores of coal cars drag along a spur to unload tons of coal at the power plant. Inside the plant are machines that grind the coal into baby-powder-fine coal dust. That dust is thrown into a furnace that thrusts itself up thirty stories in an enormous building. It creates super-heat. That heat, in turn, boils water into superheated steam. In the middle of the thirty-story building is an electrical power generator. All that coal in all that building creates all that heat in order to turn all that water into all that super-hot steam to turn a generator that is not even 1% of the size of the gigantic power plant. An incredible amount of power is poured into a relatively tiny machine.

That giant machine is a parable for the power that God Himself pours into the life of the man who surrenders to Him. Colossians 1:11 promises that you may be "strengthened with all power, according to his glorious might." That is, God continuously pours into you power that is in proportion to His own glorious might. That is like putting the ocean in a thimble. That is like putting the Grand Canyon into a child's sandbox. All the creative power of the God Who created the universe is available to be poured into your inner person. Wrap your mind around that, if you can.

But what does God expect you to do with it? Perform in the decathlon? Be an Olympic weight lifter? Will God send you on an heroic ministry trip around the world, withstanding persecution and enduring imprisonment? That is not His plan. What does He intend to do with all that power? It takes all that power to give you steadfastness, patience, and inner joy (Colossians 3:11). It takes all the power God can pour into your inner being for you to persevere, be patient with the folks who irritate you, and live with a sense of flourishing joy. God's power is available to conquer everything inside of you before He expects to use His power to perform mighty deeds outside of you. Like the tiny generator in the Muleshoe power plant, all the energy available to God Himself ceaselessly pours into your inner life to make you patient, kind, persevering, and joyful.

The greatest need for God's power is not for you to do the gigantic, dramatic deed of Christian mission. The huge need for God's power is the amount of power it takes to conquer your impatience, your lack of sticking to it, and your sadness. It takes gigantic, kinetic, active divine power to make you patient, longsuffering, and joyful. It is like putting Niagara Falls into your bathtub. Yet God continuously offers you that resource.

Why then, you must ask, do you not experience that power?

You do not experience it because you do not reckon that it is there. You live like a man with a new Mercedes 550s with its 400-horsepower motor who insists on getting out and pushing the car rather than starting the massive motor. You would rather exhaust yourself using your strength than appropriate the massive power that is available to you. The wise person would avail himself of that power.

As the great Dutch Christian, Corrie ten Boom, would say, "Nestle, don't wrestle." Most Christians live far beneath the empowerment that God must give. They do so because they do not appropriate the power that is right there waiting for them. How much of God's power are you not using?

Does the person in the next cubicle drive you crazy making weird noises? You have all the power of God Himself to treat that person with patience. Your wife meets you at the door with a whining complaint about the kids after the boss has screamed at you all day. You have the power that created the universe at your disposal to listen with kindness. Someone tags you with a cursing, obnoxious, and undeserved slight. You have the energy of a billion suns to shake it off. That is the promise of God to the man of God. You do not even have to try. Just relax into the power that God is already giving you. Reckon that you have His power and you do. You do not have to work it out; let Him live it out through you. That is the saving life of Christ within you.

When the power of the Holy Spirit fell on the church at Pentecost, wind and fire filled the room and the believers were suddenly empowered. They did not have to work it up. They did not have to moan and groan and strain to have the power. It was the gift of God given to them by His grace and for their power and use. That is exactly the way the power of God is available to you this very moment. Act on it. Reckon that it is there. Appropriate it by simply claiming it. You have won the divine lottery for power. You already have the ticket. Just turn it into heaven and let the wealth of God's power flow through you. He is ready to blow like a wind, glow like a fire, and flow like a river for you right now. He is your power plant.

PAUSE TO PONDER
Acts 1 :8

"…but you will receive power when the Holy Spirit has come upon you; and you shall be My witnesses both in Jerusalem and in all Judea, and Samaria, and as far as the remotest part of the earth."

MONDAY

First thing Monday morning, when your eyes open and your feet hit the floor, repeat to yourself, "All the power that created the universe is available for me right now." Claim it.

TUESDAY

When someone at work irritates you, do not chaff and curse under your breath. Say to God and to yourself, "I claim the power that created the universe to give me endless patience with this person right now." See what God does.

WEDNESDAY

When you are depressed, down, and devoid of any peace, reckon that God has the power already within you to give you joy and make you flourish. Tell the Lord, "I appropriate your peace right now." Lean into it and see what God does.

THURSDAY

When you cannot go on another hour, reckon that you have an endless and bottomless well of perseverance that is as energetic as God Himself. Act on it.

FRIDAY

Turn to someone who is discouraged and witness to the power that God gives you. Encourage them. Bolster them up. Pray that they will experience the endless reservoir of God's power right now, amid their situation, not after it is over. Stand with them in solidarity to claim the energy of the universe. Let them know that the very power that raised Christ from the dead is theirs this moment.

DON'T SAY "UNCLE"

When I was a boy and fighting on the playground the stronger kid would taunt the weaker kid, "Say Uncle.' If you said "uncle," the bully would generally let you go. Only later have I wondered why you had to say "uncle." Why couldn't you call on your great aunt, second cousin, or brother? There seem to be two theories. Generally, it means to give up and call on an authority figure to help. Or there is even a more classical theory. In the Roman world the uncle of man was a person of honor and virtually on the level with the father. The Latin word *patrue* means "uncle." To say to the Roman who had you cn the ground in a stranglehold *patrue* was to admit that he had more honor than you did.

Someone or something in your life will always beckon you to say "uncle." Some men say it at the first sign of trouble. Others give up in the middle of the battle. Still others hold out and when the fight is almost finished say "uncle" just before they would have won.

What situation or person makes you want to say "uncle"? The

easiest thing in the world is to give up. Anyone can give up at any time. Schubert's 8th Symphony is called "The Unfinished Symphony." For whatever reason, he gave up. You can see the score on the internet…it just stops. PhD programs are littered with folks who are ABD. That awful acronym means "all but dissertation." They finished a m aster's d egree. T hey e nrolled in a PhD. They did 48 hours of doctoral seminars. They took comprehensive exams at the highest level. Then they never wrote a dissertation. In west Fort Worth, I drove by an unfinished house many times; it's been there for decades. In Avignon, France, there is half a bridge; it goes halfway over the river. There is a biography of President John F. Kennedy called *An Unfinished Life*.

The Christian life is one of perseverance. Jesus clearly said in the first Gospel, "He who perseveres to the end shall be saved" (Matthew 24:13). The Christian life belongs to those who stick to it. At the end of *Pilgrim's Progress*, Bunyan indicated that just at the very gate of the Celestial City, there is a way to the City of Destruction. The man who believes is the man who persists. When metal workers want to temper steel they thrust it into brine or oil. Heated hot and thrust into the solution again and again tempers it, making it able to hold the edge that cuts.

The same is true of a man's life. Life will put you into the fire. The old hymn "How Firm a Foundation" says,

> "When through fiery trials thy pathway shall lie,
> My grace, all sufficient, shall be thy supply.
>
> The flame shall not hurt thee I only design
> thy dross to consume thy gold to refine.

Limp clay beside the potter's wheel is useless; it is only when it feels the fire of the kiln that the clay becomes useful. So also your life.

The Greek word for perseverance is *hupomone*. It is a combination of the preposition *hupo* and the verb *menien*. It means, literally, to remain under the load. Life will load you up; that is life. The man who does not say "uncle" is the man who stays under the load, triumphantly. Your life should not be just surviving barely but thriving triumphantly under the load. Robert Vaughn might have been "The Man from Uncle" but you must not be the man to "Cry Uncle!" Stay the course.

PAUSE TO PONDER
DEUTERONOMY 31 :8

"And the Lord is the one who is going ahead of you; He

will be with you. He will not desert you or abandon you.

Do not fear and do not be dismayed."

MONDAY

Identify one area in your life where right now, today, you want to
give up. Ask yourself why, when, and how you want to give up?
Hand it to God and ask Him to give you the grace to go on.

TUESDAY

Study the life of someone who did not give up. Theodore
Roosevelt is a great study. He overcame asthma, a bad heart,
the loss of his first wife, and blindness in one eye to be one of
the greatest examples of perseverance in history.

WEDNESDAY

Get a concordance and look up everywhere in the Bible the
word "perseverance" appears. Meditate on those verses.

THURSDAY

Reflect on one time in your life when you did not give up.
What did that do for the rest of your life?

FRIDAY

Get out of yourself by turning to someone who is tempted to
give up and stand with them, goad them on, challenge them,
help them with the load. Do something to keep someone else
from giving up. It will help you not to give up.

THE TELL ALL REVENGE: IS IT WORTH IT?

The local bar on the corner of any town, big or small, has heard its share of bad jokes and soap opera tales. The locker room at the fitness center reveals something someone else told in secret. The country club ninth hole hears enough sex scandals and juicy rumors to write a series complete with seasons 1-3 for reality television. Men who have lived through seven presidents and four wars know that some placid places hide secrets. Until they don't.

Sex scandals have permeated our society and captivated just about everyone who has a phone these days. We've watched the uncovering and undoing of many professional athletes, Hollywood stars and mongrels, politicians and even ministers.

You don't have to wait for the Sunday paper to come anymore to find out what happened on Thursday; it will pop up on your newsfeed before daylight on Friday. And, if that's not enough, we can really indulge in the "juicy details" on a new Documentary on

ESPN, Netflix, Hulu or Prime video.

Being a pastor for over 22 years, I have been privy to many a "private, – then, not- so-private" story in someone's personal life. When in hopes that the incident would remain in secret, many times the scandalous was accidentally revealed and became known to all. What might have been fact was clothed with a distortion of truth and lies. The entire family, church, organization or team is then "rocked" by such revelations.

Most often, secret sins are revealed in order to get even or gain some form of revenge by one party. The victim or participant in the specific sin wants to "'tell all'" so as to set the record straight. Usually it's the truth teller vs. the liar. The honest in one corner and the dishonest in another. The guilty vs. the innocent and every other combination in between.

I remember the words of the Lord Jesus, "Nothing is covered up that will not be revealed or hidden that will not be known. Therefore, whatever you have said in the dark shall be heard in the light, and what you have whispered in private rooms shall be proclaimed on the housetops" (Luke 12:2-3).

These words were spoken to a crowd of disciples and regular folks in Judea. They seem to be true of every one of us, then and now. Secrets will be outed. I know there are some views of the judgment that saved folks will be exempt from this. The Blood will cover all. I sure hope so, but these verses do not suggest that this is the case. I am saved, but when this happens, I may feel I got singed awhile just to straighten me out for eternity. These are a couple of verses shrouded in mystery. We will not know until we are there, but it kind of sounds like a lot of things whispered in the men's grill will get shouted all over heaven. God help us all.

The Big Fisherman, Peter, who had a lot of sin to cover, wrote the churches, "Above all, love each other deeply, because love covers over a multitude of sins" (I Peter 4:8). The wisest king of all wrote, "Hatred stirs up conflict, but love covers over all wrongs" (Proverbs 10:12). I am not totally certain what these words mean, but the "Revised Swan Version" says, "Love never makes you want to tell all to get revenge".

Ephesians 4:25 says, "Speak the truth to one another".

I want to ask you a few questions. Are you in a dilemma, wondering if you should tell someone's secret or not? Or, do you deserve for someone to out every secret you have in order to hurt you?

And, will God bless my actions, my deceit, or my manipulation of the truth?

Jesus gave us a great example of how He covered up some sins of His own followers. Just because it was more important to love them than to make them pay for those mistakes. Peter denied Him three times and cussed the last time. Yet when the Risen Christ encountered Peter on the lakeshore of Galilee, He did not say, "Peter, you're pretty worthless, how could you deny me like that after all I've done for you?" Not at all. He told Peter, "Feed my sheep."

When Jesus had the perfect revenge moment He did not use it. He appealed to the best in Peter. He did not expose; He restored.

If you claim to be a Christ follower, you can do the same.

Always be truthful, but not willing to share a secret to get revenge. Sure it's hard. But don't wait until the situation is too big to turn back. One of my favorite quotes from Max Lucado's book, *Just Like Jesus* is simply this: "The ripple of today's lie is tomorrow's wave and next year's flood".

PAUSE TO PONDER
Luke 12 :2-3

"But there is nothing covered up that will not be revealed, and hidden that will not be known. [3] Accordingly, whatever you have said in the dark will be heard in the light, and what you have whispered in the inner rooms will be proclaimed on the housetops."

MONDAY

Ponder your own secrets that you don't want to be made
public at any cost. Sit and soak in them for a while. That is not
a room for a Christian to live in, but a hallway to pass through.

TUESDAY

About whom do you know secrets that could hurt or destroy?
What have you done with those secrets? What will you do?
At work or play, have you ever taken the role to prevent
someone's secret being told in a harmful way? Have you
intervened? Did you protect? Imagine handing them over to
Jesus with the request, "Lord, these are yours.
You deal with them."

WEDNESDAY

Examine your heart and ask yourself the tough questions.
Am I being completely honest with myself, my wife, my kids,
my closest buddies? Are my business dealings marked with
truthfulness? If someone came to me for advice, would I be
candid with them to prevent them from doing something
they might regret?

THURSDAY

Do you protect someone when he tells you his biggest secret?
Can you keep it? If not, are you man enough to hand
it over to Jesus?

FRIDAY

This is the hardest thing: Can you lose the bitterness over
people who have not been truthful with you, or who have told
your secrets? To remain bitter is to drink poison and hope the
other person dies.

ENCOURAGE THE ENCOURAGERS

Matt Snowden is pastor of First Baptist Church, Waco, Texas. He is an encourager and teaches others to encourage. When he came to the church as a younger man from Mississippi, he met a legendary Waco physician and longtime member of the church, Dr. Red Covington. At the doctor's ranch, leaning on a fence post, the old doc told Matt a story.

When the famed Scottish preacher Peter MacLeod came to the church in the 1960s, an old member of the church said to the young doctor Red Covington, "A preacher needs a good friend. I am too old to be Peter's friend, but you are the same age and can be his friend." Red took that advice to heart. He became the encourager and best friend to his young pastor Peter MacLeod. They were friends from the 60s until rather recently, when they have both gone to heaven.

But here is the rest of the story. When Matt came to First Waco,

Red did the same thing for Matt that the old member had done for him nearly a half century earlier. Red told a class of younger members, "One of you need to be a friend to Matt. Every pastor needs a friend." One of those young men became the best friend to the pastor. That is what I mean by being an encourager of the encourager.

You can never know what a word of encouragement spoken in one generation may do fifty years later. The right word at the right time to the right person can last a lifetime, or two, in this instance. Few people need your criticism. I am frankly not even sure that there is such a thing as constructive criticism. I have never heard much of it. But there is such a thing as constructive encouragement. Hebrews 3:13 tells us to encourage one another daily.

Ponder that for a moment. It is a reciprocal word. If I encourage you, you are to encourage me. It works like a boomerang. When you send encouragement out it comes back to in the strangest ways as encouragement boomeranging back to you. It may be from the person you encouraged, or it may be from someone else. God has a way of presiding over all of that, but it works. Try it and you will find out.

Also, this is to be a daily habit. Don't worry about whether it works or not or whether you do it right. Just do it. Halitosis is better than no breath at all. Start it in your own home. Husbands and wives should encourage one another. Parents and children should do the same. Incidentally, part of that is your own being willing to receive encouragement. There are people so jaded that they interpret encouragement as strategy to get something from them. If someone encourages you, receive it in good faith and with joy.

Move on from your own house to work, neighbors, and for sure to pastors and workers at your church. Today pastors are subject to relentless criticism. Decide to be Red Covington to your pastor and expect nothing but appreciation in return. You do not have to be the pastor's pet. Be sensitive to people around you who need to be encouraged.

There is a great deal written today about "mindfulness." A lot of this is half-baked Buddhism. That is not what I am writing about. I am writing about old-fashioned dime-store attention to other people. Does this person in front of me need encouragement?

Years ago, it was found out that radio waves never totally disappear. They increase the further they go out at the inverse of the square. That means they never vanish. Somewhere out there in the universe Matt Dillon is still talking to Festus and Lucy is still making chocolates. Those words will never totally go away, just get fainter. Encouragement is like that. An act of encouragement will go on and on, even if it gets fainter. There is one place it will be heard: at the judgment seat of Christ (2 Corinthians 5:10).

PAUSE TO PONDER
I Thessalonians 3 :12-13

"…and may the Lord cause you to increase and overflow in love for one another, and for all people, just as we also do for you; [13] *so that He may establish your hearts blameless in holiness before our God and Father at the coming of our Lord Jesus with all His saints."*

MONDAY

Think of a specific person who encouraged you a long time ago. Ponder that person. Thank God for him or her.

TUESDAY

Recall the people you have encouraged. What did it do for them and for you?

WEDNESDAY

Spend the day consciously looking for people to encourage. Make it the goal of the day to encourage someone about something

THURSDAY

Pray for the person you encouraged, even if it is the person at the checkout in the grocery store or the person at the dry cleaners (most of them are cranks, like you an me, and need it).

FRIDAY

Encourage an encourager. Share this week with some you know and ask them to do the same.

PICK YOUR FIGHTS

When you stand before the Lord, do you want to tell Him, "Lord, I did my best to spend my last years fighting with people on Facebook about other people I do not know"?

You may want to think twice about that if those are to be your first heavenly words to the Lord. Everybody seems to be offended by just about everybody about everything. I am a Texan, born and bred. There was a Texas Baptist pioneer leader named J. B. Cranfill. He was in an all-out theological war with another Baptist. On a train through East Texas, they got into a tussle. Cranfill was so angry he shot the train! Nobody knows for sure if he was a bad aim or just got so mad, he had to shoot something. He had to apologize just to continue as a leader.

The Apostle Paul in Holy Scripture did not say, "Insofar as possible, find something to argue about with everybody you know." That would be found in the Revised Slandered Version. What Paul did say was, "If possible, so far as it depends on you, live in peace with all people" (Romans 12:18). One of our Lord Jesus' eight Beatitudes is so simple: "Blessed are the peacemakers. They shall be called the children of God" (Matthew 5:9). Do you want to be known as God's child? Make peace as much as possible.

First, I have never seen a fight lead anyone to Christ. Hot words, mad words, and hurtful words do not lead others to Christ. They do just the opposite. Conflicts seldom if ever lead anyone to come to Christ. Can you think of any?

Also, angry confrontations grieve the Holy Spirit. When you are angry and fighting, the Spirit takes a vacation from your life. The fruit of the Spirit is love, joy, and peace. The Spirit flees a life, a family, and a church that is always fighting. I understand that friendships, marriages, and churches face hard discussions. Yet such discussions can be conducted in a spirit of calmness, quietness, and forbearance. I know persons who have had to talk about the very hardest things in life without losing it.

In the 19th century the famous British preacher Charles Haddon Spurgeon out of conviction entered a huge public battle over doctrinal questions. On the other side of the battle were John Clifford and Archibald Cox. Their theology was the opposite of Spurgeon's. Even though they had a public battle over important doctrines, they remained personal friends. Even a fight over the faith does not have to break relationships. When the infamous, sensationalistic "Texas Tornado" J. Frank Norris attacked both my alma maters, he privately regretted to his secretary that he missed the friends he had alienated by his hostile tactics.

Recently President George W. Bush and Ellen DeGeneres sat

together at a Cowboy's game in Jerry Jones' box. They talked and joked. On Facebook everybody got mad, on the left and on the right. The liberals berated her and the right-wing berated Bush for sitting with her. I have a Greek word for that: CHILL. When the Apostle Paul was imprisoned at Caesarea, he did not tell the Roman leaders Felix and Festus where to go and how to get there. He reasoned with them and ingratiated himself in order to win them. If everybody is mad at everybody, there is no way on earth to tell the gospel to another person.

Let's get real. Look from the back of your hearse. The limo behind will have six friends who will carry you to your gravesite. On the way to the cemetery do you want this conversation:

"One thing you can you say about Bubba is that he never backed down from a fight," Claude observed. Rex chimed in, "Yep. When he turned against you it was all over. Never stopped being mad."

Claude coughed and said chuckling to himself, "Bubba's probably raising cane with the first person he met in heaven. He'll fight with the person in the grave next to him."

If that's how you want to be remembered, I've got a good counselor to recommend.

PAUSE TO PONDER
Colossians 3 :13

"…bearing with one another, and forgiving each other,

whoever has a complaint against anyone; just as the Lord

forgave you, so must you do also."

MONDAY

Consider two kinds of men you have known: those who always
wind up in conflict and those who make peace. How do you
feel in their presence? How do others feel?

TUESDAY

Review scenes from your own past. How did you feel
after an angry, broken relationship? How did you feel
after you made peace?

WEDNESDAY

Consider today the place, people, and times where you could
be a peacemaker. Think of scenes from home, work, and
church where you could step in with a healing word.

THURSDAY

Plan your day to find one situation today where you will make
peace. You do not know yet what it will be. Someone mad at
the grocery store. A student creating a scene in a class.
A coworker in the next cubicle. Plan how to practice
being a peacemaker today.

FRIDAY

This is tough to do. It may mean having to apologize to
someone whom you have a conflict with. Ask God to give
you the strength to be a person of peace.

SHOOT AN ARROW
INTO THE FUTURE

It may surprise you, but yours truly was a Greek major at Baylor. I studied with one of the great characters at the school, an old curmudgeon named Dr. Cutter.   One semester we translated Homer.   That is 3,000-year-old Greek.   That semester seemed about that long.   In one of the stories, Odysseus, the Arnold Schwarzenegger of his day, had to prove who he was to his wife, Penelope.   He had been gone so long she forgot what he looked like. That has not happened yet to my wife Lauree, but who knows. Anyway, to prove who he was, Odysseus shot an arrow through a hole in twelve axe heads lined up one beside the other.   That is a hard act to follow, or a hard axe to follow.

There are some great arrow stories in the Bible.   When God wanted to take out the awful King Ahab, he used a pagan Syrian soldier to shoot an arrow without aiming, and it found the chink in Ahab's armor.   It shot him dead (1 King 22:34).   God guided the arrow and it was His instrument of judgment against an awful king. In another passage, however, there is a redemptive use of arrow shot.

The prophet Elisha was dying (2 Kings 13 14-17). The sorry, weak, spineless king, Joash, went to see the dying prophet. He was a sorry king from a sorry family. He went to see Elisha in the same way a lot of politicians showed up at Billy Graham's funeral. It was good to be associated with Elisha. The old prophet revived at the visit and told King Joash, "Take a bow and arrows." The king took out his personal bow and some arrows. Then the old prophet put his feeble, ancient hands on the young hands of the king. Then Elisha told King Joash, "Open a window eastward." The surprised king opened the window. Then the old prophet said, "Shoot." And the king shot the arrow, guided by the gnarled hands of the prophet. The arrow was aimed in the direction of the enemies of God's people. The prophet cried out, "The Lord's arrow of victory!" Together the two shot an arrow into the future. The arrow both participated in and started the Lord's victory.

In a sense all of us have the opportunity to shoot an arrow into the future. We can do something today that can have a huge outcome in the future. The life of faith is a life of willingness to shoot arrows into the future. When a couple marries, they are shooting an arrow into the future. When you start a degree, you are shooting an arrow into the future. When you risk starting a new business, you shoot an arrow into the future. Any time we act today believing that God will give the victory in some tomorrow, we shoot an arrow into the future.

After World War II, the Baptist Christian layperson Truett Cathy wondered what he would do. In 1946, Truett Cathy opened a tiny diner called the Dwarf Grill in Hapeville, Georgia. It was in this diner where Truett developed the signature sandwich and the quality service for which the family-owned business is known. He called it "Dwarf Grill" because the place was so small, The company tested 1,200 different ways to cook the chicken sandwich. His first attempt at a second location failed. His partner and brother died in a crash. Truett kept on shooting arrows into the future. This Christian company, always closed on Sunday, is now a $1.6 billion empire. It all started with Truett behind the counter in a tiny grill. He shot an arrow into the future and kept on shooting arrows into the future. He could have stopped when the second location did not work. He could have quit when he lost his brother. He kept shooting arrow into the future.

A burned-out cynic might say, "That is just one story out of thousands that flopped." I would ask this question: How many more Truett Cathy's might be out there if they had not stopped? It is the start that stops most stuff. A sure way to have no future is to stop shooting arrows of hope and aspiration into the future. Van Cliburn started playing the piano by learning where middle C was. Somebody handed Tom Brady a football and he kept on throwing it. Arnold Palmer grew up with a dad who kept the grass green on the golf course. He decided he would pick up a golf club. Out of that came his own career, but much more than that. Before Arnold, golf was a game for the elite. When he started busting golf balls with his huge forearms, every working guy in the country started to think, "I can do that." Because of Arnold, golf moved out of the country club to the muni courses.

That all happened because Arnold shot an arrow into the future and believed he could play on golf courses as surely as his father kept one.

During the last week of reading and thinking about this book, I say unto you what Elisha said to the king: SHOOT.

PAUSE TO PONDER
PHILIPPIANS 3 :12-14

"Not that I have already grasped it all or have already

become perfect, but I press on if I may also take hold of

that for which I was even taken hold of by Christ Jesus. [13]

Brothers and sisters, I do not regard myself as having taken

hold of it yet; but one thing I do: forgetting what

lies behind and reaching forward to what lies ahead, [14]

I press on toward the goal for the prize of the upward

call of God in Christ Jesus."

MONDAY

What opportunity do you have right now that requires you to charge into the future with faith? A family, a degree, a career, a goal to pump iron, lose weight, get a promotion? Identify where you need to shoot an arrow into the future.

TUESDAY

Do something concrete, definite, and measurable today to shoot an arrow into your future. Fill out an application, make a call, send an email, or sign a paper.

WEDNESDAY

Pick up some idea from your past that you never acted on. Commit yourself to do the will of God about it. Pray, pause, and then push.

THURSDAY

Recall those times in the past when you risked shooting an arrow into the future. What was the outcome when God blessed?

FRIDAY

Get beside some other soul and encourage him to act on his dreams. Virtually everyone who shoots an arrow into the future has a mentor.

ABOUT THE AUTHOR

Dennis Swanberg served the local church in pastoral ministry for twenty-three years. Then, in 1995, Dennis took a leap of faith when he stepped down as church pastor and stepped up to the microphone. Soon, the Swan became "America's Minister of Encouragement," a job he takes seriously as he continues to speak to over a hundred and fifty churches and organizations every year. He has hosted two successful TV series, authored nine books, and created over two dozen video projects.

Dennis is a graduate of Baylor University, where he majored in both Greek and Religion (1976). He earned both a Master of Divinity (1980) and a Doctor of Ministry (1986) at Southwestern Seminary, Fort Worth, Texas.

Dennis has been married to Lauree Alica Wilkes of Fort Worth for over forty years. He also has two grown sons, Chad and Dustin, a daughter-in-law Britny, and two grandchildren, Andrew James and Maxine. The Swanbergs make their home in Granbury, Texas.

If you would like to book Dr. Swanberg to speak for your church, organization, or corporate group, please feel free to contact him by email at **swanbergministries@gmail.com**. You can also begin the process of booking "the Swan" on his website, **www.dennisswanberg**.com. There you can find Dr. Swanberg's other books and products as well.

A BRIEF WORD ABOUT SWANBERG CHRISTIAN MINISTRIES

I sincerely hope that this book, *Breakfast, Bible and Bull*, has been a blessing and encouragement to you as you have read through every page. It is our prayer that you find STRENGTH for today, HOPE for tomorrow, and GRACE for every moment.

If the Lord ever directs you to help us at SCM in our "Ministry of Encouragement," just know that we appreciate your consideration. Swanberg Christian Ministries is a non-profit ministry, and we seek to encourage the saints "now that His day is drawing near" (Hebrews 10:25). We also have strong mission ties and partnerships with specific missionary evangelists in Southeast Asia and the Philippines, as well as general missions associated with other evangelical mission groups.

One of biggest blessings is continuing to encourage our United States military. The Lord has directed our paths to Iraq, Germany, South Korea, and the Middle East. Doors have continued to open at many military bases and hospitals stateside as well. We are honored for every opportunity we have to encourage an uplift those who sacrifice so much for our freedom.

Swanberg Christian Ministries
www.dennisswanberg.com
swanbergministries@gmail.com